CAMBRIDGE LIBRARY COLLECTION

Books of enduring scholarly value

Printing and Publishing History

The interface between authors and their readers is a fascinating subject in its own right, revealing a great deal about social attitudes, technological progress, aesthetic values, fashionable interests, political positions, economic constraints, and individual personalities. This part of the Cambridge Library Collection reissues classic studies in the area of printing and publishing history that shed light on developments in typography and book design, printing and binding, the rise and fall of publishing houses and periodicals, and the roles of authors and illustrators. It documents the ebb and flow of the book trade supplying a wide range of customers with products from almanacs to novels, bibles to erotica, and poetry to statistics.

Early Printed Books

Edward Gordon Duff (1863–1924) was a bibliographer and librarian with a particular interest in early printed books. He was librarian of the John Rylands Library, Manchester, from 1893 to 1900, and Sandars Reader in Bibliography at Cambridge in 1899, 1904 and 1911. Alongside research and writing he also did freelance cataloguing. Duff's work set new standards of accuracy in bibliography, which he considered a science. *Early Printed Books* was published in 1893 as part of A.W. Pollard's series 'Books about Books', and became a standard work on the subject. Duff provides a concise and clear account of the development of printing and its spread from Germany across Europe, country by country, deliberately highlighting some of the less well known aspects of the subject. The book ends with chapters on bookbinding and on the collection and description of early printed books.

T0370664

Cambridge University Press has long been a pioneer in the reissuing of out-of-print titles from its own backlist, producing digital reprints of books that are still sought after by scholars and students but could not be reprinted economically using traditional technology. The Cambridge Library Collection extends this activity to a wider range of books which are still of importance to researchers and professionals, either for the source material they contain, or as landmarks in the history of their academic discipline.

Drawing from the world-renowned collections in the Cambridge University Library, and guided by the advice of experts in each subject area, Cambridge University Press is using state-of-the-art scanning machines in its own Printing House to capture the content of each book selected for inclusion. The files are processed to give a consistently clear, crisp image, and the books finished to the high quality standard for which the Press is recognised around the world. The latest print-on-demand technology ensures that the books will remain available indefinitely, and that orders for single or multiple copies can quickly be supplied.

The Cambridge Library Collection will bring back to life books of enduring scholarly value (including out-of-copyright works originally issued by other publishers) across a wide range of disciplines in the humanities and social sciences and in science and technology.

Early Printed Books

E. GORDON DUFF

CAMBRIDGE
UNIVERSITY PRESS

CAMBRIDGE UNIVERSITY PRESS

Cambridge, New York, Melbourne, Madrid, Cape Town, Singapore,
São Paolo, Delhi, Dubai, Tokyo, Mexico City

Published in the United States of America by Cambridge University Press, New York

www.cambridge.org
Information on this title: www.cambridge.org/9781108026741

© in this compilation Cambridge University Press 2011

This edition first published 1893
This digitally printed version 2011

ISBN 978-1-108-02674-1 Paperback

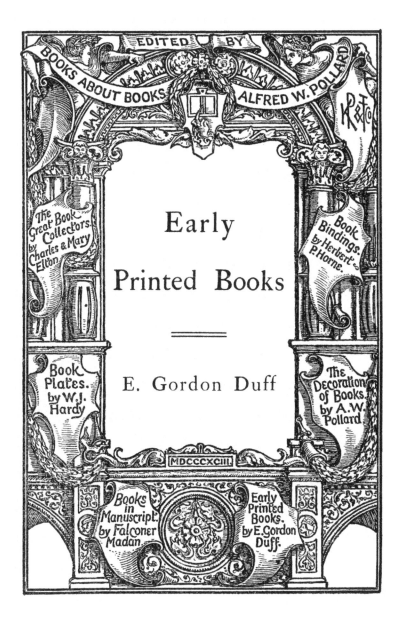

BOOKS ABOUT BOOKS

EDITED BY ALFRED W. POLLARD

The Great Book Collectors. by Charles & Mary Elton.

Book Bindings. by Herbert P. Horne.

Early

Printed Books

E. Gordon Duff

Book Plates. by W.J. Hardy

The Decoration of Books. by A.W. Pollard

MDCCCXCIII.

Books in Manuscript. by Falconer Madan

Early Printed Books. by E. Gordon Duff.

E igit̄ clemētissime pr̄
pr̄ iḣesū ẋp̄m filiū tuū
d̄ñm nostrū supplices
rogamus ac ptimus·
vti accepta habeas et
bñdicas·ḣec do ✠ na·
ḣec mu ✠ nera·ḣec sancta ✠ sacrificia il-
libata, I n pmis que tibi offerim⁹ pro
ecclia tua sancta katholica· quā pacificae·
custodire·adunare·⁊ regē digneis·toto
orbe terrar̄·vna cū famło tuo Papa no-
stro· N̄·et rege ñro· N̄·⁊ antistite nostro
N̄·⁊ oīnibꝫ orthodoxis·atꝗ katholice et
apostolice fidei cultoribꝫ.
Ẽmento dñe famulor̄ famularꝗꝗ
tuarū· N̄·ḣic fit memoria viuor̄·
et oīm circūastānū quor̄ tibi fides cogni
ta est et nota deuoco pro quibꝫ tibi offeri
mus·vel qui tibi offerūt ḣoc sacrificium

Early Printed Books

By

E. Gordon Duff

London

Kegan Paul, Trench, Trübner & Co., Ltd.

MDCCCXCIII

TO

THE MEMORY OF

HENRY BRADSHAW

———

ἀποθανὼν ἔτι λαλεῖ

Preface

IN the following pages I have endeavoured to give a short account of the introduction of printing into the principal countries and towns of Europe, and to bring our information on the subject as far as possible up to date.

Small books on large subjects are for the most part both superficial and imperfect, and I am afraid the present book forms no exception to this rule, but my excuse must be that I have attempted rather to draw attention to more out of the way information than to recapitulate what is already to be found in the majority of bibliographical books.

Above all, I have tried as far as possible to confine myself to facts and avoid theories, for only by working from facts can we help to keep bibliography in the position, to which Henry Bradshaw raised it, of a scientific study.

And, in the words of a learned Warden of my own college, 'if any shall suggest, that some of the inquiries here insisted upon do seem too minute and trivial for any prudent Man to bestow his serious thoughts and time about, such persons may know, that the discovery of the true nature and cause of any the most minute thing, doth promote real knowledge, and therefore cannot be unfit for any Man's endeavours who is willing to contribute to the advancement of Learning.'

I must express my best thanks to two friends, Mr. F. J. H. Jenkinson, University Librarian, Cambridge; and Mr. J. P. Edmond, Librarian to the Earl of Crawford and Balcarres, for very kindly reading through the proofs of the entire book and making many useful suggestions and corrections.

E. G. D.

March 1893.

Contents

PAGE

CHAPTER I

STEPS TOWARDS THE INVENTION, ... 1

CHAPTER II

THE INVENTION OF PRINTING, ... 21

CHAPTER III

SPREAD OF PRINTING IN GERMANY, ... 39

CHAPTER IV

ITALY, ... 59

CHAPTER V

FRANCE, ... 78

CHAPTER VI

THE LOW COUNTRIES, ... 95

CHAPTER VII

SPAIN AND PORTUGAL—DENMARK AND SWEDEN, . . 113

CHAPTER VIII

WESTMINSTER : CAXTON—WYNKYN DE WORDE—JULIAN
NOTARY, ... 125

PAGE

CHAPTER IX

Oxford and St. Alban's, ... 147

CHAPTER X

London : John Lettou — William de Machlinia —
Richard Pynson, ... 160

CHAPTER XI

The Spread of the Art in Great Britain, . . 174

CHAPTER XII

The Study of Bookbinding, ... 185

CHAPTER XIII

The Collecting and Describing of Early Printed
Books, ... 201

Index of Printers and Places, ... 213

Illustrations

PAGE FROM THE CANON OF THE MASS PRINTED BY
SCHOEFFER ABOUT 1458 (*much reduced*),   *Frontispiece*

(From the unique copy in the Bodleian.)

PLATE   PAGE

I. PAGE 3 OF THE 'MIRABILIA ROMÆ,'   .   .   .   11

(From the copy in the British Museum.)

II. THE CATALOGUE ISSUED BY SCHOEFFER ABOUT 1469
(*reduced*), ...   31

(Reproduced from a full-sized facsimile of the original
in the Munich Library, published in the *Centralblatt
für Bibliothekswesen*.)

III. PAGE 3 OF THE 'LIBER EPISTOLARUM' OF GASPARINUS
BARZIZIUS, the first book printed at Paris,   .   .   .   83

(From the copy in the British Museum.)

IV. FRAGMENT OF AN EDITION OF THE 'DOCTRINALE' OF
ALEXANDER GALLUS, one of the so-called 'Costeriana,'   98

(Reduced from the copy in the British Museum.)

V. PAGE OF THE FIRST EDITION OF THE 'SARUM BREVIARY,'   127

(Printed at Cologne about 1475.)

VI. PART OF A PAGE FROM THE 'GOLDEN LEGEND,'   .   .   144

(Printed by Julian Notary in 1503. From the copy in
the British Museum.)

PLATE   PAGE

VII. First page of the 'Excitatio ad Elemosinam
     Faciendam,' 152

     (Printed at Oxford about 1485. From the unique copy
     in the British Museum.)

VIII. Page of the 'Horæ ad Usum Sarum,' . . . 163

     (Printed at London by Machlinia. From the fragment
     in the University Library, Cambridge.)

IX. Last page of the 'Festum Nominis Jesu,' . . 167

     (Printed at London by Pynson about 1493. From the
     unique copy in the British Museum.)

X. Stamped Binding with the Device of Pynson, . 193

     (From the original in the British Museum.)

EARLY PRINTED BOOKS.

CHAPTER I.

STEPS TOWARDS THE INVENTION.

WHEN we speak of the invention of printing, we mean the invention of the art of multiplying books by means of single types capable of being used again and again in different combinations for the printing of different books. Taking the word printing in its widest sense, it means merely the impression of any image; and the art of impressing or stamping words or pictures seems to have been known from the very earliest times. The handles of Greek amphoræ, the bases of Roman lamps and vases, were often impressed with the maker's name, or other legend, by means of a stamp. This was the basis of the art, and Cicero (*De Nat. Deorum*, ii. 37) had suggested the combination of single letters into sentences. Quintilian refers to stencil plates as a guide to writing; and stamps with letters cut in relief were in common use amongst the Romans. The need for the invention, however, was not great, and it was never made. The first practical printing, both from blocks and movable type, was done in China. As early as A.D. 593 the more important texts were printed from engraved wooden plates by the order of the Emperor Wên-ti, and in the eleventh century printing from movable type was introduced by a certain smith named Picheng. The multiplicity of Chinese characters rendered the discovery of movable type of little economical value, and the older system of block printing has found favour even up to the present time. In the same way, Corea and Japan, though both had experimented with movable type, returned to their former custom of block printing.

It is impossible now to determine whether rumours of the art could have reached Europe from China, and have acted as incentives to its practice. Writers on early printing scout the idea; and there is little to oppose to their verdict, with our present uncertain knowledge. Modern discoveries, however, point to the relations of China with foreign countries in the fourteenth century having been much more important than is generally supposed.

The earliest productions in the nature of prints from wooden blocks upon paper which we find in Europe, are single sheets bearing generally the image of a saint. From their perishable nature but few of these prints have come down to our times; and though we have evidence that they were being produced, at any rate as early as the fourteenth, perhaps even as the thirteenth century, the earliest print with a definite and unquestioned date still in existence is

the 'St. Christopher' of 1423. This print was discovered in 1769 by Heinecken, pasted inside the
binding of a manuscript in the library of the Convent
of the Chartreuse at Buxheim in Swabia. The manuscript, which is now in the Spencer Library,[1] is
entitled *Laus Virginum*, is dated 1417, and is said
to have been given to the Monastery of Buxheim by
a certain Anna, Canoness of Buchau, 'who is known to
have been living in 1427.' On the inside of the other
board of the binding is pasted a cut of the Annuncia-
tion, said to be of the same age and workmanship as
the St. Christopher. It is worth noticing that there
seem to have been some wood engravers in this
Swabian monastery, who engraved the book-plate for
the books given by 'Dominus Hildibrandus Branden-
burg de Bibraco' towards the end of the fifteenth
century ; and these book-plates are printed on the
reverse sides of pieces of an earlier block-book, very
probably engraved and printed in the monastery for
presentation to travellers or pilgrims.

The date on the celebrated Brussels print of 1418
has unfortunately been tampered with, so that its
authenticity is questioned. The print was found by
an inn-keeper in 1848, fixed inside an old chest, and
it was soon acquired by the Royal Library at Brussels.

---

[1] The Spencer Library has now passed into the possession of Mrs.
Rylands, of Manchester ; but as many of the early printed books in it
are described in Dibdin's *Bibliothecâ Spenceriana*, and as it is so
widely known under the name of the Spencer Library, it has been
thought best, in order to avoid confusion, to refer to it under its old
name throughout the present book.

Since the date has been touched up with a pencil, and
at the same time some authorities consider 1468 to
be the right reading, it is best to consider the St.
Christopher as the earliest dated woodcut. Though
these two are the earliest dated prints known, it is,
of course, most probable that some others which are
undated may be earlier; but to fix even an approximate date to them is in most cases impossible.
The conventional way in which religious subjects
were treated, and the extraordinary care with which
one cutter copied from another, makes it difficult even
for a specialist to arrive at any very definite conclusions.

In England, wood engraving does not seem to have
been much practised before the introduction of printing, but there are one or two cuts that may be
assigned to an earlier period. Mr. Ottley, in his
Inquiry concerning the Invention of Printing, drew
attention to a curious Image of Pity which he had
found sewn on the blank leaf at the beginning of
a manuscript service-book. This cut, of which he
gives a facsimile in his book, is now in the British
Museum. Another cut, very similar in design and
execution, and probably of about the same date, was
found a few years ago in the Bodleian, also inserted
at the beginning of a manuscript service-book. In
the upper part of the cut is a half-length figure of
our Lord, with the hands crossed, standing in front
of the cross. On a label at the top of the cross is
an inscription, the first part of which is clearly O

BACIΛEVC, but the second part is not clear. In the British Museum cut it has been read 'hora 3ª;' and though this interpretation is ingenious, and might be made to fit with the Museum copy (which has unfortunately been touched up), the clearer lettering of the Bodleian copy, which has evidently the same inscription, shows that this reading can hardly be accepted.

Below the figure we have the text of the indulgence—

'Seynt gregor' with othir' popes & bysshoppes yn feer
Have graunted' of pardon xxvi dayes & xxvi Mill' yeer'
To theym that befor' this fygur' on their' knees
Deuoutly say v pater noster & v Auees.'

Ottley was of opinion that his cut might be of as early a date as the St. Christopher; but that is, of course, a point impossible to determine. From the writing of the indulgence, Bradshaw considered it to belong to the northern part of England; and the subject is differently treated from other specimens of the Image of Pity issued subsequently to the introduction of printing, for in them the various symbols of the Passion are arranged as a border round the central figure. Inserted at the end of a Sarum Book of Hours in the British Museum is a drawing of an Image of Pity, with some prayers below, which resembles in many ways the earlier cuts.

The woodcut alphabet, described by Ottley, now in the British Museum, has been considered to be of English production, because on one of the prints is written in very early writing the two words 'London' and 'Bechamsted.' There seems very little reason beyond this for ascribing these letters to an English workman, though it is worth noticing that they were originally bound up in a small volume, each letter being pasted on a guard formed of fragments of English manuscript of the fifteenth century.

In the Weigel Collection was a specimen of English block-printing which is now in the British Museum ; it is part of some verses on the Seven Virtues, but it is hard to ascribe any date to it. Another early cut is mentioned by Bradshaw as existing in Ely Cathedral. It is a cut of a lion, and is fixed against one of the pillars in the choir, close to the tomb of Bishop Gray, whose device it represents. This bishop died in 1479, so that an approximate date may be given to the cut. It is very probable that these last two specimens of block-printing are later than the introduction of printing into England, and the only ones that should be dated earlier are the British Museum and Bodleian Images of Pity.

A good many single woodcuts were executed in England before the close of the fifteenth century. They were mostly Images of Pity, such as have been mentioned, or 'rosaries' containing religious emblems, with the initials I. H. S. A curious cut in the Bodleian represents the Judgment, and below this a body in a shroud. Above the cut is printed, 'Surgite mortui Venite ad Judicium,' and below on either side of a shield the words, 'Arma Beate Birgitte De Syon.'

A curious devotional cut is inserted in the *Faques Psalter* of 1504 in the British Museum, containing the emblems of the Passion and a large I. H. S. At the base of the cut are the initials d. h. b., perhaps referring to the place where the cut was issued. Most of these cuts were doubtless produced in monasteries or religious houses to give or sell to visitors, who very often inserted them in their own private books of devotion, and in this manner many have been preserved. The Lambeth copy of the Wynkyn de Worde *Sarum Horæ* of 1494 shows signs of having contained eighteen of such pictures, though only three are now left.

After the single leaf prints we come to the block-books, which we may look upon in some ways as the precursors of printed books.

' A block-book is a book printed wholly from carved blocks of wood. Such volumes usually consist of pictorial matter only ; if any text is added in illustration, it likewise is carved upon the wood-block, and not put together with movable types. The whole of any one page, sometimes the whole of two pages, is printed from a single block of wood. The manner in which the printing was done is peculiar. The block was first thoroughly wetted with a thin watery ink, then a sheet of damp paper was laid upon it, and the back of the paper was carefully rubbed with some kind of dabber or burnisher, till an impression from the ridges of the carved block had been transferred to the paper. Of course in this fashion a sheet could only be printed on one side; the only block-book which does not possess this characteristic is the *Legend of St. Servatius* in the Royal Library of Brussels, and that is an exceptional volume in many respects besides.'[1] These block-books must be considered as forming a distinct group of themselves, radically different from other books, though undoubtedly they gave the idea to the inventor of movable type. They continued to be made during the whole of the fifteenth century, almost always on the same plan, and each one as archaic looking as another. The invention of movable type did not do away with the demand, and the supply was kept up.

Unfortunately we have no data for determining the exact period at which these books were made; and it is curious to note that all the editions which are dated have a late date, the majority being between 1470 and 1480, and none being earlier than the first date, with the exception of the Brussels block-book, which is dated 1440.

The number of different block-books in existence is hard to estimate, but it must approach somewhere near one hundred. Many of these are of little importance, many others of too late a date to be of much interest.

The best known of the earlier block-books are the *Ars Moriendi*, the *Biblia Pauperum*, the *Apocalypse*, and the *Canticum Canticorum*. Of these, the first and third are probably German, the second and fourth Dutch.

[1] Conway's *Woodcutters of the Netherlands*. Cambridge, 1884. 8vo.

Of all these books there are a number of editions, not easily distinguishable apart, and which it is difficult to place in chronological order. These editions are hardly editions in the modern sense of the term. They were not produced by a printer who used one set of blocks till they were worn out, and then cut another. The woodcutter was the only tradesman, and he sold, not the books, but the blocks. He cut set after set of blocks to print the few books then in demand, and these were sold to private purchasers. We find wealthy people or heads of religious establishments in possession of such sets. In the inventory of Jean de Hinsberg, Bishop of Liège, 1419–1455, are noticed—

'Unum instrumentum ad imprimendas scripturas et ymagines

'Novem printe lignee ad imprimendas ymagines cum quatuordecim aliis lapideis printis.'

Thus, these editions do not necessarily follow one another ; some may have been produced side by side by different cutters, others within the interval of a few months, but by the same man. Their date is another difficult point. The copies of the *Biblia Pauperum*, *Apocalypse*, and *Ars Moriendi*, which belonged to Mr. Horn, were in their original binding, and it was stamped with a date. The books were separated and the binding destroyed. Mr. Horn asserted from memory that the first three figures of the date were certainly 142, and the last probably an 8. Mr. Conway very justly points out that the resemblance of a 5 of that date to our 2 was very strong, and that Mr. Horn's memory may have deceived him.

It will be noticed in examining block-books generally, that the letterpress in the majority of the later examples is cut in imitation of handwriting, and not of the square church hand from which printing types and the letterpress of the earlier block-books were copied. The reason of this probably is, that it was found useless to try to compete with the books printed from movable type in regularity and neatness. To do so would have involved a much greater expenditure of trouble by the woodcutter and designer. The illustrations were the important part of the book, and the letterpress was put in with as little trouble as possible.

The sheets on which the early block-books were printed were not quired, *i.e.* placed one inside the other to form a quire or gathering, as was done in ordinary printed books, but followed each other singly. In many of the books we find signatures, each sheet being signed with a letter of the alphabet as a guide to the binder in arranging them.

Among the dated block-books may be mentioned an edition of the *Endkrist*, dated 1472, produced at Nuremberg ; an edition of the *Ars Moriendi* cut by Hans Sporer in 1473 ; and another of about the same period cut by Ludwig zu Ulm. Of the *Biblia Pauperum* there are three dated editions known, one of 1470 and two of 1471. A copy of the *De generatione Christi* has the following full colophon :—

IMPIVM   ROMA

Oma ciuitas scta
Caput mundi
Von anbeginne
der welt dz cccc
vnd l iare do throia
erstoret ward von
dem krichischem kayser vnd
die fursten vnd hern fluhen
von der grossen stat throia
auf dem mere mit grossem
guet in andre land vnd dm den

'Johannes Eysenhut impressor, anno ab incarnationis dominice M° quadringentesimo septuagesimo 1°.' Hans Sporer of Nuremberg produced an edition of the *Biblia Pauperum* in 1475, and Chatto speaks of another of the same year without a name, but containing as a mark a shield with a spur upon it, which he supposes to stand for the name Sporer. Many of these later books were not printed in distemper on one side of the paper only, but on both sides and in printer's ink, showing that the use of the printing press was known to those who produced them.

Among the late block-books should be noticed the *Mirabilia Romæ* [Hain 11,208]; for why it should have been printed as a block-book is a mystery. It consists of 184 pages of text, with only two illustrations, printed on both sides of the page, and evidently of late date. The letterpress is not cut in imitation of type, but of ordinary handwriting, and the book may have been made to sell to those who were not accustomed to the type of printed books. The arms of the Pope which occur in the book are those of Sixtus IV., who occupied the papal chair from 1471 to 1484, so that the book may be considered to have been produced within those two dates, probably nearer the latter. The accompanying facsimile is taken from the first page of text.

The best known of the block-books, and the one which has the most important place in the history of printing, is the *Speculum Humanæ Salvationis*. While it is called a block-book, it has many differences from those we have previously spoken of, and occupies a position midway between them and the ordinary printed book.

The earliest block-books were printed page by page, and the sheets were bound up one after the other ; but the *Speculum* is arranged in quires, though still only printed on one side of the page. In it, too, the text is, as a rule, printed from movable type, except in the case of one edition, where some pages are entirely xylographic. There are four editions known, printed, according to the best authorities, in the following order :—

1. Latin, printed with one fount. [Hessels, 2.]

2. Dutch, printed with two founts. [Hessels, 3.]

3. Latin, with twenty leaves printed xylographically. [Hessels, 1.]

4. Dutch, with one fount. [Hessels, 4.]

In all these four books the same cuts are used, and the type with which they were printed was used in other books.

Edition 1 contains sixty-four leaves, made up by one gathering of six leaves, three of fourteen, and one of sixteen ; the text is throughout printed from movable type. In two copies, those in the Meerman-Westreenen Museum at the Hague, and the Pitti Palace at Florence, are to be found cancels of portions of some leaves. Either the text or the illustration has been defectively printed ; in each case the defective part has been supplied by another copy pasted on.

Edition 2 contains sixty-two leaves, made up in

the same way as the first edition, but having only four leaves in the first gathering. Two leaves in this edition are printed in a different type from the rest of the book.

Edition 3 contains the same number of leaves, and is made up in the same way as edition 1. It is remarkable for having twenty leaves printed entirely from blocks, text as well as illustrations.

Edition 4 is made up in the same way as edition 2. The copy in the library at Lille contains some leaves with text printed upon both sides, seemingly by an error of the printer. The very fact of their existence shows that it was possible to print the text on both sides of the leaf. There must therefore have been some reason other than the ignorance or incapacity of the printer for printing these books on one side only, or, as it is called, anopisthographically.

There can be very little doubt that Mr. Sotheby is correct in his conjecture, that 'the then usual process of taking off the wood engravings by friction, rendered it impossible to effect two impressions back to back, as the friction for the second would materially injure the first. On this account, and on no other, we presume, was the text printed only on one side.' In the Lille copy above mentioned, two leaves, 25 and 26 (the centre sheet of the third quire), contain printed on their other side the text, not the illustrations, of leaves 47 and 62 (the first sheet of the fifth quire.

From this we learn three things of great importance—1. That the text and the cut were not printed at the same time, and that the text was printed first. 2. That the printer could print the text, for which he used movable type, on both sides of the paper. 3. That the book was printed, not page by page, but two pages at a time.

Mr. Ottley was strongly of opinion, after careful examination, that the book was certainly printed two pages at a time. He says, 'The proofs of this are, I think, conclusive. The upper lines of the text in those two pages always range exactly with each other. . . . Here and there, in turning over the book, we observe a page printed awry or diagonally on the paper; in such case, if the other page of the same sheet be examined, the same defect will be noticed. Upon opening the two Dutch copies of the edition, which I shall hereafter show to be the fourth at Harlem, in the middle sheet of the same gathering we find, upon comparing them, the exact same breadth and regularity of the inner margin in both, and the lines of the two pages range with each other exactly the same in both copies, which could not be the case had each page been printed separately.'

Where and when was this book printed? Conjectural dates have been given to it ranging from 1410 to 1470. The earliest date that can be absolutely connected with it is 1471–73. Certainly there is nothing in its printing which would point to its having been executed earlier than 1470. Its being printed only on the one side of the leaf was a matter of necessity on account of the cuts, and is not a sign of remote age, while the printing of two pages at a time argues an advance of knowledge in the printer, and consequently a later date. About 1480–81 the blocks which had been used for the four editions of the *Speculum* passed into the hands of John Veldener. This Veldener printed in Louvain between 1475 and 1477, and he was not then in possession of the blocks. ' At the end of 1478 he began work at Utrecht, still, however, without this set of blocks. For his second edition of the *Fasciculus temporum*, published 14th February 1480, he had a few new blocks made, some of which were copied from *Speculum* cuts. At last, on the 19th April 1481, he published an *Epistles and Gospels* in Dutch, and into that he introduced two cut-up portions of the real old *Speculum* blocks. This was the last book Veldener is known to have printed at Utrecht. For two years we hear nothing more of him, and then he reappears at Kuilenburg, whither he removed his presses. There, on the 27th September 1483, he printed a quarto edition of the *Speculum* in Dutch. For it he cut up all the original blocks into their separate compartments, and thus suited them to fit into the upper portion of a quarto page. He had, moreover, twelve new cuts made in imitation of these severed portions of the old set, and he printed them along with the rest. Once more, in 1484 he employed a couple of the old set in the Dutch *Herbarius*, which was the last book known to have been issued by him at Kuilenburg. Thenceforward the *Speculum* cuts appear no more.'[1]

The only place, then, with which the *Speculum* blocks are definitely connected is Utrecht, and there they must be left until some further evidence is forthcoming respecting their origin; nor have we any substantial reason for believing that when they passed into the possession of Veldener they had been. in existence for more than ten or twelve years.

Some among the late block-books are of interest as having been produced by men who were at the same time printers in the ordinary sense of the word. There is part of a *Donatus* in the Bodleian, with a colophon stating it to be the work of Conrad Dinckmut, a printer at Ulm from 1482 to 1496. In the British Museum is a German almanac of about 1490 produced by Conrad Kacheloffen, who printed a number of books, many with illustrations, at Leipzig. For a book so small as the *Donatus*, a book which was always in demand, it would be almost as economical to cut blocks as to keep type standing, and we consequently find a number of such xylographic editions produced at the very end of the fifteenth century. In the Bibliothèque Nationale are two original blocks, bought by Foucault, the minister of Louis XIV., in Germany, and probably cut about 1500 or shortly before. The letters are cut in exact imitation of type, and with such regularity that a print from the block might almost pass for a print

[1] Conway's *Woodcutters*, p. 13.

from ordinary type, did not the bases and tops of a few letters overlap.

The latest block-book of any size was printed at Venice. It is the *Figure del Testamento Vecchio*, printed about 1510 by Giovanni Andrea Vavassore.

In the library at Lambeth Palace are two curious block-printed leaves of early English work. Each leaf contains an indulgence printed four times, consisting of a figure of Saint Cornelius and five lines of text. 'The hole indulgence of pardon granted to blessed S. Cornelis is vi score years, vi score lentes, ii M ix C and xx dais of pardon for evermore to endure.'

It shows us very clearly the cheapness with which such work could be produced; for, in order to save the time which would be occupied in taking impressions singly from one block, two blocks have been used almost exactly the same, so that two impressions could be taken off at once. This was usually done in printing indulgences from movable type, for there the trouble of setting up twice was very small compared to the gain in the time and labour which resulted from it.

There still remains to be noticed the one specimen of xylography produced in France. This is known as *Les Neuf Preux*. It consists of three sheets of paper, each of which contains an impression from a block containing three figures. They are printed by means of the frotton in light-coloured ink, and have been coloured by hand. The first sheet contains

B

pictures of the three champions of classical times, Hector, Alexander, and Julius Cæsar; the second, the three champions of the Old Testament, Joshua, David, and Judas Maccabæus; the third, the three champions of mediæval history, Arthur, Charlemagne, and Godfrey of Boulogne. Under each picture is a stanza of six lines, all rhyming, cut in a bold type.

These leaves form part of the *Armorial* of Gilles le Bouvier, who was King-at-Arms to Charles VII. of France; and as the manuscript was finished between 9th November 1454 and 22nd September 1457, it is reasonable to suppose that the prints were executed in France, probably at Paris, before the latter date. The verses are, at any rate, the oldest printed specimen of the French language.

When we consider that printing of a rudimentary kind had existed for so many centuries, and that during the whole of the early part of the fifteenth century examples with words or even whole lines of inscription were being produced, we can only wonder that the discovery of printing from movable types should have been made so late. It has been said inventions will always be made when the need for them has arisen, and this is the real reason, perhaps, why the discovery of printing was delayed. The intellectual requirements of the mediæval world were not greater than could be satisfactorily supplied by the scribe and illuminator, but with the revival of letters came an absolute need for the more rapid multiplication of the instruments of learning. We may even say that the intellectual activity of the fifteenth century not only called printing into existence, but furnished it with its noblest models. The scholarly scribes of Italy at that epoch had revived the Caroline minuscules as used in the eleventh and twelfth centuries, and it was this beautiful hand which the early Italian printers imitated, thereby giving us the 'Roman' type in which our books are still printed.

I cannot more fitly close this preliminary chapter than by quoting from the MS. note-books of Henry Bradshaw the opening sentences of his article 'Typography' for the *Encyclopædia Britannica*, an article which unfortunately was never completed.

'Typography was, in the eyes of those who first used it, the art of multiplying books, of writing by means of single types capable of being used again and again, instead of with a pen, which, of course, could only produce one book at a time.[1]

'The art of multiplying single sheets, for which woodcut blocks could be used to serve a temporary purpose, may be looked upon as an intermediate stage, which may have given the idea of typography. When the reproduction of books had long passed out of the exclusive hands of the monasteries into the hands of students or hangers-on of the universities, any invention of this kind would be readily and

---

[1] This is clearly brought before us by the words of the first printers at Avignon, 'ars artificialiter scribendi,' a phrase used several times over in speaking of their new invention.

rapidly taken up. When there was no Greek press in Paris, we find Georgius Hermonymus making a living by constant copying of Greek books for the scholars who were so eager for them. So Reuchlin in the same way supported himself by copying.

'In fact, the two departments of compositor and corrector in the printing office were the direct representatives and successors of the scribe and corrector of manuscripts from the early times. The kind of men whom we find mentioned in the early printing offices as correctors, are just such men as would be sought for in earlier times in an important scriptorium. In our modern world, printed and written books have come to be looked upon as totally distinct things, whereas it is impossible to bring before our minds the state of things when books were first printed, until we look upon them as precisely the same. They were brought to fairs, or such general centres of circulation as Paris, Leipzig, or Frankfort, before the days of printing, just as afterwards, only that printing enabled the stationer to supply his buyers with much greater rapidity than before, and at much cheaper rates ; so that the laws of supply and demand work together in such a manner that it is difficult to say which had more influence in accelerating the movement.'

CHAPTER II.

THE earliest specimen of printing from movable type known to exist was printed at Mainz in 1454. In making this statement, I do not wish to pass over the claims of France and the Low Countries to the invention of printing, but only to point out that, in considering the question, we must put the evidence of the printed books themselves first, and then work from these to such documentary evidence as we possess. France has the documents but no books; the Low Countries neither the one nor the other; and therefore, if we are to set about our inquiries on any rational plan, we must date the invention of printing from the date of its first product. This is the famous *Indulgence* of Nicholas V. to such as should contribute money to aid the King of Cyprus against the Turks.

In the copy of the *Indulgence* now preserved in the Meerman-Westreenen Museum at the Hague (discovered by Albert Frick at Ulm in 1762, and afterwards in the collections of Schelhorn and Meerman), the place of issue, Erfurth, and the date, November 15, have been filled in; thus giving us as the earliest authentic date on a printed document, November 15, 1454.

In the years 1454 and 1455 there was a large demand for these *Indulgences*, and seven editions were issued. These may be divided into two sets, the one containing thirty-one lines, the other thirty lines ; the first dated example belonging to the former.

These two sets are unmistakably the work of two different printers, one of whom may well have been Peter Schœffer, since we find the initial letters which are used in the thirty-line editions used again in an *Indulgence* of 1489 certainly printed by him. Who, then, was the printer of the other set ? He is generally stated to have been John Gutenberg ; and though we have no proof of this, or indeed of Gutenberg's having printed any book at all, there is a strong weight of circumstantial evidence in his favour.

What do we know about John Gutenberg, the presumed printer of the first dated specimen of printing ? The earliest information comes from the record of a lawsuit brought against him at Strasburg in 1439 by George Dritzehn, for money advanced.

There is hardly room for doubt that the business on which Gutenberg was engaged, and for which money was advanced him, was printing. There is a certain ambiguity about some of the expressions, but the greater part of the account is too clear and straightforward to allow of any doubt.[1]   It may

---

[1] A very careful literal and unabridged translation will be found in Hessels' *Gutenberg*, pp. 34–57. The text used is Laborde's with some

safely be said that before 1439 Gutenberg was at work at Strasburg, experimenting on and perfecting the art of printing.

The next document which relates to him as a printer is the lawsuit of 1455, the original transcript of which was recently found at Göttingen. This was brought against him by Fust to recover a loan of 800 guilders. In this lawsuit mention is made of two of Gutenberg's servants, Heinrich Keffer, afterwards a printer at Nuremberg, and Bertolf von Hanau, supposed to be the same as Bertold Ruppel, the first printer at Basle. Peter Schœffer also appears as a witness. We learn from this suit that somewhere about August 1450, Fust advanced the amount of 800 guilders, and about December 1452 a like amount; but these loans were advanced in the first instance by Fust towards assisting a work of which the method was understood, and we are therefore justified in considering that by that time Gutenberg had mastered the principles of the art of printing.

The first two books printed at Mainz were the editions of the *Vulgate*, known from the number of lines which go to the page as the forty-two line and thirty-six line Bibles. The forty-two line edition is generally called the Mazarine Bible, because the copy which first attracted notice was found in Cardinal

corrections, and Schœpflin's readings when they vary are given in notes. It should be noted that Mr. Hessels implies that the account of this trial is a forgery, or at any rate unreliable; but his negative and partial reasoning cannot stand against the evidence brought forward by many trustworthy authorities.

Mazarin's library; and the thirty-six line edition, Pfister's or the Bamberg Bible, because the type used in it was at one time in the possession of Albrecht Pfister of Bamberg. On the question as to which of the two editions is the earlier, there has been endless controversy; and before going farther, it will be as well to state shortly the actual data which we possess from which conclusions can be drawn.

The Paris copy of the forty-two line Bible has the rubricator's inscription, which shows that the book was finished before the 15th August 1456.

The only exact date we know of, connected with the other Bible, is 1461, this date being written on a copy of the last leaf, also preserved in the Bibliothèque Nationale at Paris.

The types of both Bibles were in existence in 1454, for they were used in the thirty and thirty-one line letters of *Indulgence* printed in that year.

The type of the forty-two line Bible is clearly a product of the Gutenberg-Fust-Schœffer partnership, for it is used afterwards by Schœffer as Fust's partner, and must therefore have been the property of Fust. Mr. Hessels, who has worked out the history of the types with extreme care and accuracy, says: 'I have shown above that one of the initials of the thirty line *Indulgence* is found in 1489 in Schœffer's office. The church type of the same *Indulgence* links on (in spite of the different capital P) to the anonymous forty-two line Bible of 1456. This Bible links on to the thirty-five line Donatus, which is in the same type, and has

Schœffer's name and his coloured capitals.[1] This again brings us to the *Psalter*, which Joh. Fust and Peter Schœffer published together on the 14th August 1457, at Mentz, their first (dated) book with their name and the capitals of the *Donatus*.'

We may safely say of the forty-two line Bible, that it could not have been begun before about August 1450 (when Gutenberg entered into partnership with Fust), and that it could not have been finished later than August 1456 (the rubricated date of the Paris copy).

As regards the thirty-six line Bible, M. Dziatzko has brought forward, after much patient study, some remarkable evidence. He proves, from an examination of the text, that the thirty-six line Bible was set up, at any rate in part, from the forty-two line Bible. One copy survives which betrays this ; for the compositor has passed from the last word of leaf 7 to the first word of leaf 9. In another place he has misread the beginning of a chapter, and included the last two words of the one before, which is explained by the arrangement of the text in the forty-two line edition.

Dziatzko concludes that this latter edition was the product of the Gutenberg-Fust confederation, and that Gutenberg may have produced the thirty-six line Bible more or less *pari passu*, either alone or in partnership with (perhaps) Pfister. An examination

---

[1] The colophon of this book says : . . . ' per Petrum de Gernssheym in urbe Moguntina cum suis capitalibus absque calami exaratione effigiatus ;' and Mr. Hessels translates ' cum suis capitalibus,' ' with his capital letters,' a rendering which is surely impossible.

of the paper used in printing the two books points to the conclusion that there were substantial means available for the production of the forty-two line Bible, while the thirty-six line seems to show many separate purchases of small amounts of different papers.

It is impossible 'to assign any date for the commencement of the thirty-six line Bible. Fust had clearly nothing to do with it, and the type may have been made and some sheets printed before the partnership for printing the forty-two line Bible was entered into in 1450. The largeness of the type and consequent lesser number of lines to the page points to an early date, for the tendency was always to increase the number of lines to the page and economise paper. Thus we find that when the first gathering of the forty-two line Bible had been printed, which has only forty lines to the page, the type was recast, so as to have the same face of letter on a smaller body ; and with this type the page was made to contain forty-two lines to the page.

The workmanship and the appearance of the type would also lead us to suppose that the thirty-six line Bible was printed earlier than the *Manung widder die Durcke*, which, being an ephemeral publication applicable only to the year 1455, must presumably have been printed in 1454.

We can therefore probably put both Bibles earlier than 1454.

The first book with a printed date is the well-known *Psalmorum Codex* of 1457, printed by Schœffer. Of this book nine copies are known, and all vary slightly from each other.[1] Only two types are used throughout the *Psalter*, but both are very large. Mr. Weale, on account of the variations observable in the letters, insists that the book was printed from cut and not cast type ; but he gives no reason for this opinion ; and when we consider that books had already been produced from cast type, it is impossible to understand why Schœffer should have resorted to so laborious a method. The dissimilarity of some letters is not so strong a proof of their having been cut, as the similarity of the greater number is of their having been cast. Bradshaw, who was of this opinion, had also noted some curious shrinkages in the type, resulting from the way the matrices for the type were formed.

The most striking thing about the *Psalter* are the wonderful capital letters ; and how these were printed has always been a vexed question. In the editions of 1457 and 1459 they are in two colours, the letter in one colour and the surrounding ornamentation in another. Though it is impossible to determine exactly how they were produced, there is at any rate something to be settled on the question. In one case, in the edition of 1515, in which these initials were still used, the exterior ornament has

[1] For a very full account of this book see the Catalogue of MSS. and Printed Books exhibited at the Historical Music Loan Exhibition, by W. H. James Weale, London, 1886, 8vo, pp. 27-45.

been printed, but the letter itself and the interior
ornament have not. This shows at any rate that the
letter and the ornament were not on one block, and
that the exterior and interior ornaments were on
different blocks; and is also in favour of the sugges-
tion put forward by Fischer, that the ornament and
the letter, though on different blocks, were not
printed at the same time. In support of his theory,
Fischer mentioned a case of the letter overlapping
the ornament in a copy of the edition of 1459, and
such a slip could not have occurred had the letter
and ornament been printed from inset blocks in the
method now known as the Congreve process.

It has also been argued by some writers, among
whom is William Blades, that the letter was not
printed in colour, but that the design was merely
impressed in blank upon the paper or vellum, and
afterwards filled in with colour by the illuminator.
This is shown, it is said, by some portions of lines
here and there in the ornamentation remaining
uncoloured, a result surely due to imperfect inking
rather than to a careless illuminator. It is hardly
probable that the rubricator would begin a line and
leave the end uncoloured while it was plainly traced
for him ; but, on the other hand, it is just such a fault
as would, and often did, occur in printing an elaborate
and involved ornament. No doubt in some cases the
capitals, like the letters of the text, were touched up
by the rubricator; and this is, as a rule, most noticeable
when the ornament or letter is in blue. The blue

ink used had a green tinge, and in some cases looked
almost grey, and was therefore very often touched up
with a brighter colour. Mr. Weale is of opinion
that these letters were not set up and printed with
the rest of the book, but were printed, subsequently
to the typography, not by a pull of the press, but by
the blow of a mallet on the superimposed block.'

It was probably about 1458, between the times of
printing the two editions of the *Psalter*, that Schœffer
printed the book called in his catalogue of 1469-70,
Canon misse cum prefacionibus et imparatoriis suis.
This was the Canon of the Mass, printed by itself for
inserting in copies of the Missal. This particular
part, being the most used, was often worn out
before the rest of the book; and we know from early
catalogues [1] that it was the custom of printers to
print this special part on vellum. While the printing
of a complete Missal would have been a doubtful
speculation, the printing of this one part, unvarying
in the different uses, required no great outlay, and
was almost certain to be profitable. Two copies only
are known, and these are of different editions. One
is in the Bodleian, and was bound up with an
imperfect copy of the *Mainz Missal* of 1493. The
other is in the Imperial Library at St. Petersburg,
in a copy of the *Breslau Missal* of 1483.

The Bodleian copy consists of twelve leaves,

---

[1] In a catalogue issued by Ratdolt about 1491 we read : . . . 'vide-
licet unum missarum (?) in papiro bene corporatum et illigatum cum
canone pergameneo non ultra tres florenos minus quarta : sed cum
canone papireo duos florenos cum dimidio fore comparandum.'

printed on vellum in the large type of the *Psalter*, and ornamented with the same beautiful initials. The capital T of the *Te igitur*, commencing the Canon, is as large as the well-known B of the *Psalter*, and even more beautiful in execution. Besides the ordinary coloured capitals which occur also in the *Psalter*, there is a monogram composed of the letters V.D., standing for *Vere dignum.*

In 1459 a second edition of the *Psalter* was issued, and also the *Rationale Durandi*, both containing coloured capitals, though some copies of the latter book are without the printed initials. A *Donatus* without date, printed in the type of the forty-two line Bible, has also the coloured capitals, and may be dated before 1460. After that time we only find these letters in use for the editions of the *Psalter* which appeared in 1490, 1502, 1515, 1516; and for a *Donatus* in the 1462 Bible type. Their size and the trouble of printing them account, no doubt, for their disuse.

In June 1460, Schœffer issued the *Constitutions* of Clement V., a large folio remarkable for the care with which it was printed, and for the clever way in which the commentary was worked round the text. In 1462 appeared the first dated *Bible*, which is at the same time the first book clearly divided into two volumes.[1] In the next few years we have a number

---

[1] It has never, I think, been noticed in print that some of the capital letters in certain sheets of this Bible are not the work of the rubricator, but are printed. Attempts were made to print both the blue and the red on the same page, but it apparently was found too

Volētes sibi oparare infrascriptos libros maḡ
cū diligēria correctos. ac in hmōi lra mogunnō
impſſos. bn̄ ōtnuatoſ. vemāt ad locū habitauo:
nis infrascriptū.

Primo pulcram bibliam in pergameno,
Item ſcd̄am ſcd̄e beati thome de aquino.
Item quartū ſcriptū eiuſdē.
Itē tractatū eiuſdē de eccie ſacris a articlis fidei.
Itē Auguſtinū de doctrina xpiana. cum tabula
notabili p̄dicantib multū p̄ficua.
Itē tractatū de rōne et ōſciēra.
Itē mḡrm iobānē gerſon de cuſtodia lingue.
Itē oſolatoriū timorate ōſcie venerabilis fratris
iobānis mder ſacre theologie p̄feſſoria exami.
Itē tractatū eiuſdē de ōtractib mercatoꝛ.
Itē bullā p̄n ꝓp ſedi contra thurcos.
Itē biſtoriā de p̄ſentacōe beate marie v̄ginis.
Itē canonē miſſe cū p̄facōib a ip̄aratoꝛins ſuis.

annpboms m magna ac groſſa littera.
Itē iobannē ianuēſem in catholicon.
Itē ſextum decretaliū. Et clemētinā cum apparatu
iobannis andree.
Itē m iure ciuili. Inſtitucōnes.
Itē arbores de ōſanguitate a affimtate.
Itē libros tullii de officiis. Cū eiuſdē paradoxis.
Itē biſtoriā griſeldis. de maxia ōſtantia mlieriū
Item biſtoriam Leonardi aretum exhocatio de a:
moꝛe Tancredi filie figiſmūde m Duiſcardum.

ḩer eſt littera pſalterij

of Bulls and other such ephemeral publications, relating mostly to the quarrels which were going on in Mainz; but in 1465, Schœffer starts again to produce larger books, and in this year we have the *Decretals* of Boniface VIII. and the *De Officiis* of Cicero. This latter book is important as being the first containing Greek type, that is, if it is allowed to be earlier than the *Lactantius* of the same year printed at Subiaco. In 1466 it was reprinted.

In or about 1469, Schœffer printed a most interesting document, a catalogue of books for sale by himself or his agent. It is printed on one side of a sheet, and was meant to be fixed up as an advertisement in the different towns visited, the name of the place where the books could be obtained being written at the bottom. There are altogether twenty-one books advertised, three of which were not printed by Schœffer, but probably by Gutenberg; and there are also in the list three unknown books. Nearly all the important works from the press are in it, the 1462 Bible on vellum, the *Psalter* of 1459, the *Decretals*, the *Cicero*, and others. At the foot of the list is printed in the large *Psalter* type, 'Hec est littera psalterii,' so that the sheet is the earliest known type-specimen as well as catalogue.

laborious, and was given up. The red letters were printed in colour; the letters which were to be blue were impressed in blank, and afterwards filled up in colour by the illuminator. He did not always follow the impressed letter, so that its outline can be clearly seen. Some copies of this Bible have Schœffer's mark, and a date at the end of the first volume; others are without them. The colophons also vary.

The three books which are unknown, at any rate as having been printed by Schœffer, are the *Consolatorium timorate conscientie* and the *De contractibus mercatorum*, both by Johann Nider, a famous Dominican, and the *Historia Griseldis* of Petrarch.

In 1470, Schœffer put out another advertisement relating to his edition of the *Letters of St. Jerome*, printed in that year. Of this broadside two copies are known, one in the Munich Library, the other, formerly belonging to M. Weigel, in the British Museum. From 1470 to 1479, Schœffer printed a large number of books. Hain mentions twenty-seven, almost all of which he himself had collated. This was the busiest time in Schœffer's career, and he carried on business in several towns. His agent in Paris, Hermann de Stalhœn, died about 1474, and the books in his possession were dispersed. On the complaint of Schœffer, Louis XI. allowed him 2425 crowns as compensation,—a sum which shows that the stock of books must have been very large. In 1479 he was received as a citizen of Frankfort-on-the-Maine on payment of a certain sum, no doubt in order that he might there sell his books. At Mainz he became an important citizen, and was made a judge.

From 1457 to 1468, Schœffer had used only four types, the two church types which appear in the *Psalter*, and the two book types which appear in the *Durandus*. In this year he obtained a fifth type, like the smaller one of the *Durandus*, and about the same in body, but with a larger face. In 1484 and 1485 two new types appear, one a church type very much resembling that used in the forty-two line Bible, but with a larger face ; the other, a vernacular type, which occurs first in the *Hortus Sanitatis* of 1485, a book containing Schœffer's mark though not his name, and appears the year following in the *Breydenbach*, printed at Mainz by Erhard Reüwick. Reüwick was an engraver, and the frontispiece to the *Hortus Sanitatis* is perhaps from his hand, showing, if it be so, a connection between him and Schœffer, which his use of the latter's type tends to confirm. In fact, it seems most probable that the text of the two editions of the *Breydenbach*, the Latin one of 1486 and the German one of 1488, was really printed by Schœffer, while Reüwick engraved the wonderful illustrations. The title-page of this book is an exquisite piece of work, and by far the finest example of wood engraving which had appeared. It is further noticeable as containing cross-hatching, which is usually said to have first been used in the poor cuts of that very much overpraised book, the *Nuremberg Chronicle* of 1493. It contains also a number of views of remarkable places, printed as folded plates. Some of these views are as much as five feet long, and were printed from several blocks on separate pieces of paper, which were afterwards pasted together.

Schœffer continued to print during the whole of the fifteenth century, though towards the end he issued few books. Another printer, Petrus de Friedberg, started to print at Mainz in 1493, and between that time and 1498 issued a fair number of books. About 1480 a group of six or seven books, all un- dated, were printed at Mainz, which were long sup- posed to be very early, and not impossibly printed by Gutenberg. One of these was a *Prognostication*, said to be for the year 1460, and therefore presumably printed in 1459. A copy is preserved in the library of Darmstadt; and some years ago this was examined by Mr. Hessels, who found that the date had been tampered with, and that it should really read 1482.

From 1455 onwards, while the press of Schœffer was busily at work, we lose sight of Gutenberg. Three books, however, all printed about 1460 at Mainz, are ascribed to him. These are the *Catholicon* (a kind of dictionary) of 1460, the *Tractatus racionis et conscientiæ* of Matthæus de Cracovia, and the *Summa de articulis fidei* of Aquinas, both without date. To these may be added a broadside indulgence printed in 1461. Bernard attributes these books to the press of Henry Bechtermuntze, who afterwards printed with the same type at Eltvil. One fact appears to tell strongly against this conclusion. In 1469–70, when Schœffer issued his catalogue, we find these three books in it, the remainder being all of Schœffer's own production. How did they get into Schœffer's hands? Had they been printed by Bechtermuntze we should surely find the *Vocabularius ex quo* also in the catalogue, for he had issued editions in 1467 and 1469. It is more probable that they had formed the stock of a printer who had given up business, and had therefore got rid of all the books remaining on his hands.[1]

In the copy of the *Tractatus racionis* belonging to the Bibliothèque Nationale the following manuscript note occurs: 'Hos duos sexternos accomidauit mihi henrycus Keppfer de moguncia nunquam reuenit ut reacciperetur,' etc. This Keppfer was one of Gutenberg's workmen ; and his name occurs in the notarial instrument of 1455, so that this inscription forms a link between the book and Gutenberg.

We have, unfortunately, no direct evidence as to the printer. We know that the books were printed at Mainz, for it is directly so stated in the Schœffer catalogue and in the colophon of the *Catholicon*. Now we know of no printers at Mainz in 1460 except Schœffer and Gutenberg, and Schœffer was certainly not the printer of these books. On the other hand, there are no books except these three that could have been printed by Gutenberg ; and if these three are to be ascribed to any one else, Gutenberg is left in the position of a known printer who printed nothing. It has been shown above that it is very improbable that the books were printed by Bechtermuntze ; and the

---

[1] In 1468 all the materials connected with Gutenberg's press were handed over to Conrad Homery, their owner, who binds himself to use the type only in Mainz ; and also binds himself, if he sells it, to sell it to a citizen of Mainz, *provided that citizen offers as much as a stranger*. The stock of printed books would also belong to Homery in his capacity of creditor, and would be sold in Mainz, where, so far as we know, there was no one except Schœffer to buy them.

fact that in 1470 the remaining copies were in the
hands of a man who did not print them, points to
their real printer having died or given up business.
Though from these various facts we can prove nothing
as regards the identity of the printer, we have some
show of probability for imagining that he must have
been Gutenberg.

There is no doubt whatever that the *Catholicon*
type appears at Eltvil in the hands of the two
brothers Bechtermuntze in 1467, for in the *Vocabularius ex quo* there is a clear colophon stating that
the book was commenced by Henry Bechtermuntze
and finished by Nicholas Bechtermuntze and Wygand
Spyess of Orthenberg on the 4th of November 1467.

There has been a great deal of argument on the
question how these types came into the hands of
the Eltvil printers while Gutenberg was alive. We
know that Gutenberg became a pensioner of Adolph
II. in 1465, and would therefore presumably give up
printing in that year. The types and printing
materials which he had been using belonged to a
certain Dr. Homery, and were reclaimed by him in
1468. The distance from Eltvil to Mainz is only
some five or six miles, and the Rhine afforded easy
means of communication between the two places, so
that the difficulty of the transference of type backwards and forwards seems, as a rule, very much
overstated. Although we have no evidence of printing at Eltvil before 1467, still it will be best to give
an account of the press in this chapter, since it was

so intimately connected with the early press at Mainz.

In 1467, on the 4th November, an edition of the *Vocabularius ex quo* was published. The colophon tells us that the book was begun by Henry Bechtermuntze, and finished by his brother Nicholas in partnership with a certain Wygand Speyss of Orthenberg. A second edition was published in June 1469 by Nicholas Bechtermuntze alone. Both these editions are printed in the type used for the *Catholicon* of 1460, but with a few additional abbreviations. In 1472 a third edition of the *Vocabularius ex quo* was issued, in a type very similar to the type of the thirty-one line *Letters of Indulgence*, but slightly smaller; and an edition of the *Summa de articulis fidei* of Aquinas [Hain, *1426] was issued in the same type. In 1477 a fourth edition of the *Vocabularius ex quo* was printed by Nicholas Bechtermuntze; the type is different from that used in the other books, and is identical, as Mr. Hessels tells us, with that used about the same time by Peter Drach at Spire.

Before leaving Mainz, it will be as well to notice the books printed by the Brothers of the Common Life at Marienthal. This monastery was close to Mainz on the opposite side of the river, and not far from Eltvil. The earliest book is a *Copia indulgentiarum per Adolphum archiepiscopum Moguntinum concessarum*, dated from Mainz in August 1468, and presumably printed in the same year. In 1474 they issued the *Mainz Breviary,* a book of great rarity, and of which the copies vary ; in fact, of certain portions there seem to have been several editions. Their latest piece of printing with a date is a broadside indulgence of 1484, of which there is a copy at Darmstadt.   Dr. F. Falk, in his article ' *Die Presse zu Marienthal im Rheingau,*' mentions fourteen books as printed at this press ; but he includes some printed in a type which cannot with certainty be ascribed to Marienthal.   The Brothers seem to have used only two types, both of which are found in the *Breviary.* Both are very distinctive, especially the larger, which is a very heavy solid Gothic letter, easily distinguishable by the curious lower case *d.*

CHAPTER III.

BEFORE 1462, when the sacking of Mainz by Adolf von Nassau is popularly supposed to have disseminated the art of printing, presses were at work in at least two other German towns, Strasburg and Bamberg.

The first of these places is mentioned by Trithemius, who records that after the secret of printing was discovered, it spread first to Strasburg. Judging merely from authentic dates, this is evidently correct, for we have the date 1460 for Strasburg, and 1461–62 for Bamberg. There are, however, strong reasons for supposing that this order is hardly the correct one, and that Bamberg should come first. Since, however, the statement and the dates exist, it will be safer for us provisionally to consider Strasburg as the first, and state later on the arguments in favour of Bamberg.

Though no dated book is known printed at Strasburg before 1471, in which year Eggestein printed the *Decretum Gratiani*, and though Mentelin's first dated book is of the year 1473, yet we know from the rubrications of a copy of the *Latin Bible* in the library at Freiburg, that that book was finished, the first volume before 1460, and the second before 1461. Concerning the printer, John Mentelin, a good deal is known. Born at Schelestadt, he became a scribe and illuminator; but, like many others, abandoned the original business to become a printer. P. de Lignamine in his Chronicle says that by 1458, Mentelin had a press at Strasburg, and was printing, like Gutenberg, three hundred sheets a day. By 1461 he had finished printing the forty-nine line edition of the *Latin Bible*. He died on the 12th December 1478, leaving two daughters, one married to Adolf Rusch d'Ingwiller, his successor; the other, to Martin Schott, another Strasburg printer. Very few of his books are dated; and as his types have not yet been systematically studied, the books cannot be ranged in any accurate order.

Taking the information in Lignamine's Chronicle as exact, and we have no reason to doubt its accuracy, we may take certain books in the type of the Bible as the earliest of Mentelin's books.[1] Round 1466 we can group some other books, the *Augustinus de arte predicandi* and the *Homily on St. Matthew* by St. Chrysostom. A copy of the former book in the British Museum is rubricated 1466; and of the latter a copy in the Spencer Collection has the same year

---

[1] In the University Library, Cambridge, is a very interesting copy of the first volume of this Bible, bought at the Culemann sale. It consists for the most part of proof-sheets, and variations from the ordinary copies occur on almost every page. It is printed on small sheets of paper in the manner of a broadside, the sheets being pasted together at the inner margin.

added in manuscript. In Sir M. M. Sykes' sale was
a volume containing copies of these two books bound
together in contemporary binding. About 1470, Mentelin issued a catalogue containing the titles of nine
books, including a *Virgil*, a *Terence*, and a *Valerius
Maximus*. Mentelin also printed the first edition of
the Bible in German, a folio of 406 leaves. Several
copies are known with the rubricated date of 1466 ;
and the same date is also found in a copy of the
Secunda secundæ of Aquinas. Many other of his
books contain manuscript dates, and show that they
are considerably earlier than is usually supposed.

Henry Eggestein, whose first dated book was
issued in 1471, was living in Strasburg as early as
1442, and probably began to print almost as soon as
Mentelin. The earliest date attributable to any of
his books is 1466, the date written by Bamler, at that
time an illuminator, in the copy of one of his forty-
five line editions of the Bible now in the library at
Wolfenbüttel. In 1471, Eggestein himself tells us
that he had printed a large number of books. A
little time before this he had issued a most glowing
advertisement of his Bible. He appeals to the good
man to come and see his wonderful edition, produced,
as the early printers were so fond of saying, not by
the pen, but by the wonderful art of printing. The
proofs had been read by the best scholars, and the
book printed in the best style. This Bible, which has
forty-five lines to the column, was finished by 1466,
for the copy now in the library at Munich was

rubricated in that year.   The only printed dates that
occur in Eggestein's books are 1471 and 1472.   Hain
gives three books of the years 1474, 1475, and 1478
as printed in his type, but these contain no printer's
name.

The most mysterious printer connected with the
history of the Strasburg press, is the printer who used
a peculiarly shaped capital R, and is therefore known
as the R printer.   He seems to have been very
generally confounded with Mentelin till 1825, when
the sale catalogue of Dr. Kloss' books appeared.   In
this sale there happened to be two copies of the
Speculum of Vincent de Beauvais, one the undoubted
Mentelin edition, the other by the R printer.   The
writer of the note in the catalogue stated that, on
comparison, the types of the two editions, though very
like each other, were not the same.   Since the type is
different, and the peculiar R has never yet been
found in any authentic book printed by Mentelin, we
may safely say that Mentelin was not the printer.
To whom, then, are the books to be ascribed?   Many
consider them the work of Adolf Rusch d'Ingwiller.
M. Madden attributes them all to the Monastery of
Weidenbach at Cologne, in common with most of the
other books by unknown printers, and dates them
about 1470.   Bradshaw, writing to Mr. Winter Jones
in 1870, says: 'In turning over a volume of fragments
yesterday, I found a Bull of Sixtus IV., dated 1478,
in the type of the famous "R" printer so often confounded with Mentelin.   His books are commonly

put down to 1470 or earlier, and I believe no one
ever thought of putting his books so late as 1478.[1]
Yet this little piece is almost the only certain date
which is known in connection with this whole series
of books.' Complete sets of the *Speculum* of Vincent
de Beauvais are very often made up, partly from
Mentelin's and partly from the R printer's editions,
which points to their having been probably printed at
the same place and about the same time. The
earliest MS. date found in any of the books by the
R printer is 1464; for a note in the copy of the
Duranti Rationale divinorum Officiorum in the library
at Basle, states that the book was bought in that
year for the University. If this date is authentic,
it follows that Strasburg was the first place where
Roman type was used.

The next important printer at Strasburg is George
Husner, who began in 1476 and printed up till 1498.
His types may be recognised by the capital H, which
is Roman, and has a boss on the lower side of the
cross-bar. John Gruninger, who began in 1483, issued
some beautifully illustrated books, the most celebrated being the *Horace, Terence,* and *Boethius,* and
Brandt's *Ship of Fools.* He and another later Strasburg printer, Knoblochzer, share with Conrad Zeninger
of Nuremberg the doubtful honour of being the most
careless printers in the fifteenth century.

Albrecht Pfister was printing at Bamberg as early

---

[1] This indulgence had been noticed by Bernard, *De l'Origine de
l'Imprimerie,* vol. ii. pp. 108, 109.

as 1461, and his first dated book, Boner's *Edelstein*,
was issued on 4th February of that year. He used
but one type, a discarded fount from Mainz which
had been used in printing the thirty-six line Bible
and the other books of that group. By many he is
credited with being the printer of the thirty-six line
Bible,—a theory which a short examination of the
workmanship of his signed books would go far to
upset. Pfister seems to have been more of a wood
engraver than a printer, relying rather on the attractive nature of his illustrations than on the elegance of
his printing. We can attribute to him with certainty
nine books, with one exception all written in German,
and with two exceptions all illustrated with woodcuts.
Mr. Hessels is of opinion that certain of these books
ought to be placed, on account of their workmanship,
before the *Boner* of 1461 ; as, for instance, the *Quarrel
of a Widower with Death*, in which the lines are very
uneven. There are certain peculiarities noticeable in
Pfister's method of work which occur also in the
Manung widder die Durke, a prognostication for
1455, preserved in the Royal Library, Munich, and in
the *Cisianus zu dutsche* at Cambridge, the most marked
being the filling up of blank spaces with an ornament
of stops. The curious rhyming form of these calendars, and the dialect of German in which they are
written, resemble exactly the rhyming colophon put
by Pfister to the Boner's *Edelstein*. In all three
cases the ends of the lines are not marked, but the
works are printed as prose.

Paulus Paulirinus of Prague, in his description of
a 'ciripagus' wrote: 'Et tempore mei Pambergæ
quidam sculpsit integram Bibliam super lamellas, et
in quatuor septimanis totam Bibliam super parga-
meno subtili prcsignavit scriptura.' Some writers
have suggested that these words refer to the thirty-
six line Bible; but a 'Bible cut on thin plates' can
only be a block-book, and probably an edition of the
Biblia Pauperum. Paul of Prague composed a large
part of his book before 1463, when no other printer
besides Pfister was at work at Bamberg, and these
words probably apply to either the Latin or German
edition of the *Biblia Pauperum* which Pfister issued.

We have no information as to when or where
Pfister began to print, and the extraordinary rarity of
his books prevents much connected work upon them.
There is no doubt that he came into possession of the
type of the thirty-six line Bible, and in this type a
number of books were printed. The earliest of these
books is probably the *Manung Widder die Durke,*
which, since it was a prognostication for 1455, was
presumably printed in 1454. This book, as far as it is
possible to judge, was manifestly printed after the
thirty-six line Bible, and by a different printer. In it
we first find the peculiar lozenge-shaped ornament of
stops which continues through the series of books in
this type. The calendar of 1457 in the Bibliothèque
Nationale, probably printed in 1456, is the next piece
in the series to which an approximate date can be
given. Of this calendar, originally printed on a

single sheet, only the upper half remains, found in 1804 at Mainz, where it had been used as a cover for some ecclesiastical papers. It bears the following in-scription: 'Prebendarum. Registrum capituli ecclesie Sancti Gengolffi intra muros Moguntiæ receptorum et distributorum anno LVII., per Johan: Kess, vicarium ecclesie predicte.' Thus, at the end of the year 1457 or beginning of 1458, it was treated at Mainz as waste-paper. With this calendar may be classed the *Cisianus zu dutsche* at Cambridge, a rhyming calendar in German.

There are, then, the series of nine or ten books, usually all given to Pfister, though only two bear his name; and of these some are after and some can be placed before 1461. The typographical peculiarities of Pfister's signed books are the same as those of the early calendars, and point to his having also produced them. This brings us at once into the obvi-ous difficulties, for we should have Pfister printing as early as 1454, while Gutenberg was still in partner-ship with Fust. The knowledge about Pfister's press is too meagre to allow any of these difficulties to be cleared up, though something may yet result from a more careful examination of the books themselves. The only examples in England of books printed by Pfister (with the exception of the *Cisianus*) are in the Spencer Library. There are there four books and a fragment of a fifth.

The conjecture put forward by M. Dziatzko, that Gutenberg may have printed the thirty-six line Bible in partnership with some other printer, as, for example, Pfister, would certainly, if any proof in its favour could be adduced, simplify matters very much. We should then have all the books in a natural sequence, from the Bible to the latest books of Pfister, and we could account for the printing of the *Manung* in 1454, while Gutenberg was still in partnership with Fust and Schœffer for the production of the forty-two line Bible. The workmanship of the thirty-six line Bible is in some points different from the later books, all of which were probably the work of Pfister, who, according to this theory, must have been at work at Mainz as early as 1454. The contract between Gutenberg and Fust did not necessarily bind the former to print only with Fust, so that he may also have worked with Pfister, and taught him the art.

Pfister's last dated book, *The Histories of Joseph, Daniel, Judith, and Esther*, was printed in 1462, not long after the day of St. Walburga (May 1).

After this time we hear of no book printed at Bamberg till 1481, when John Sensenschmidt printed the *Missale Ordinis S. Benedicti*, commonly known as the Bamberg Missal.

Cologne, from its situation on the Rhine, was in a favourable position for receiving information and materials from Mainz, and we find that by 1466, Ulric Zel of Hanau, a clerk of the diocese of Mainz, was settled there as a printer. His first dated book was the Chrysostom *Super psalmo quinquagesimo ;* but some other books were certainly issued before it. The Cicero *De Officiis*, a quarto with thirty-four lines to the page, is earlier, and is perhaps the first book he issued. It has many signs of being a very early production, and may possibly have been issued before Schœffer's edition of 1465.

M. Madden, in his *Lettres d'un Bibliographe*, has argued that a very early school of typography existed at Cologne, in the Monastery of Weidenbach. Though his researches have thrown a great deal of light on various points connected with early printing, and are in some ways of real value, much that he has theorised about Weidenbach requires confirmation. We can hardly be expected to believe, as he would try to persuade us, that Caxton, and Zel, and Jenson, and many other printers whose types belong to different families, could all learn printing at this one place. It would be impossible for men who had learnt to print in the same school to produce such radically different kinds of type, and work in such different methods. The early tentative essays of Zel's press can be clearly identified, and their order more or less accurately determined, from their typographical characteristics. His earliest books were quartos; and of these the first few have four point holes to the page. These point holes are small holes about an inch from the top and bottom lines, and nearly parallel with the sides of the type, made by the four pins which went through the paper when one side of the page was printed, and served as a guide to place the paper straight when the other side was printed.[1]

Then, before he settled down to printing his quartos with twenty-seven lines to the page, he experimented with various numbers of lines. We can safely start with the following books in the following order :—

A. Cicero, *De officiis,* . . . . . 34 lines to the page.
　　Chrysostom, *Super psalmo quinquagesimo,* 1466, 33　,,　　,,
　　Gerson, *Super materia celebrationis missæ,* . 31　,,　　,,
　　　,,　　*Alphabetum divini amoris,* . . 31　,,　　,,

These form an early group by themselves, and commence on the first leaf; the second group begins with

B. Augustinus, *De vita christiana* and *De singularitate clericorum,*
　　1467, 28 and 27 lines to the page.

Then follows a number of tracts by Gerson and Chrysostom, all having four point holes, and all probably printed before 1470. Zel continued to print throughout the whole of the fifteenth century.

At a very early date there were a number of other printers settled at Cologne, all using types which, though easily distinguishable, are similar in appearance and of the same family; and their books have generally been ascribed to Zel. To many of them it is impossible to put a printer's name; and certain of them have been divided into groups known by the

---

[1] The use of four points to obtain a correct register is generally a sure sign of the infancy of a press. Blades says they are to be found in all the books printed in Caxton's Type 1.

title of the commonest book in that group which has
no edition in another group. For instance, we have
a certain number of books printed by the printer
of the *Historia Sancti Albani;* another printer is
known as the printer of *Dictys* (perhaps Arnold ther
Hoernen); another as the printer of *Augustinus de
Fide* (perhaps Goiswin Gops), and so on. No doubt,
in time, when the Cologne press has been more carefully studied, the identity of some of these printers
will be discovered; but at present there are a great
many difficulties waiting to be cleared away.

Arnold ther Hoernen, who began to print in or
before 1470, was the pioneer of several improvements.
The *Sermo ad populum,* printed in 1470, has a title-
page, and the leaves numbered in the centre of the
right-hand margin ; very soon after he printed a book
with headlines. He printed 'infra sedecim domos,'
and used a small neat device, of which there are two
varieties, always confused. John Koelhoff, a native
of Lubeck, printed at Cologne from 1472 (?) to 1493,
when he died. If the date of 1472 in his *Expositio
Decalogi* of Nider be correct, he was the first printer
who used ordinary printed signatures ; but the date of
the book is questioned. The shapes of the capital
letters in Koelhoff's types are very distinctive ; and it
is curious to notice that a fount unmistakably copied
from them was used by a Venetian printer named
John de Colonia. Nicholas Gotz of Sletzstat, who
began printing about 1470, though we find no dated
book of his before 1474, and who finished in 1480,

used a device engraved upon copper in the 'manière criblée,' or dotted style. It consists of a coat-of-arms surmounted by a helmet and crest, with his motto, 'Sola spes mea inte virginis gratia.' In some books we find the motto printed in a different form—'Spes mea sola in virginis gratia.' In 1475 was issued the *Sermo de presentacione beatissime virginis Marie*, the only book known containing the name of Goiswinus Gops de Euskyrchen. In 1476, Peter Bergman de Olpe and Conrad Winters de Homborch began to print, and were followed in 1477 by Guldenschaff, and in 1479 by Henry Quentell, the last named being the most important printer at Cologne during the latter years of the fifteenth century.

Gunther Zainer was the first printer at Augsburg; and in March 1468 issued his first dated book, the *Meditationes vite domini nostri Jesu Christi*, by Bonaventure. Some of his undated books show signs from their workmanship of having been printed at a still earlier date. At first he used a small Gothic type, but in 1472 he published the *Etymologiæ S. Isidori* in a beautiful Roman letter, the first, with a date, used in Germany. His later books are printed in a large, thick, black letter, and have in many cases ornamental capitals and borders. He was connected in some way with the Monastery of the Chartreuse at Buxheim, and to their library he gave many of his books; and we learn from their archives that he died on the 13th April 1478. By 1472 we find two more printers settled in Augsburg, John Baemler and John

Schussler. The first of these, before becoming a printer, had been a scribe and rubricator, and as such had sometimes signed his name to books. This has given rise to the idea that he printed them, and he is often quoted as the printer of a Bible in 1466. He worked from 1472 to 1495, printing a very large number of books. Schussler printed only for three years, from 1470 to 1473, issuing about eight books, printed in a curious small type, half-Gothic, half-Roman, and very like that used at Subiaco. About 1472–73, Melchior de Stanheim, head of the Monastery of SS. Ulric and Afra, purchased some presses and began to print with types, which seem to have been borrowed from other Augsburg printers, such as Zainer, Schussler, and Anthony Sorg. The latter started on his own account in 1475, and issued a very large number of books between that year and 1493.

The early Augsburg books are especially noted for their woodcuts, which, though not perhaps of much artistic merit, are very numerous and curious. Some very beautifully printed books were also produced about the end of the century by John Schœnsperger, who is celebrated as the printer of the *Theurdanck* of 1517.

In 1470, John Sensenschmidt and Henry Keppfer of Mainz, whom we have before spoken of as a servant of Gutenberg, began to print at Nuremberg. Their first book was the *Codex egregius comestorii viciorum*, and in the colophon the printer says : ' Nuremburge anno, etc., LXX° patronarum formarumque concordia et proporcione impressus.' These words are exactly copied from the colophon of the *Catholicon*, which is considered to have been printed by Gutenberg.

In 1472, Frederick Creusner and Anthony Koburger, the two most famous Nuremberg printers, both began to print. They seem to have been closely connected in business, and we sometimes find Creusner using Koburger's type; for instance, the *Poggius* of 1475 by Creusner, and the *Boethius* of 1473 by Koburger, are in the same type. Most of the early Nuremberg types are readily distinguished by the capital N, in which the cross stroke slants the wrong way. Koburger was perhaps the most important printer and publisher of the fifteenth century. He is said to have employed twenty-four presses at Nuremberg, besides having books printed for him in other towns. About 1480 he issued a most interesting catalogue, of which there is a copy in the British Museum, containing the titles of twenty-two books, not all, however, printed by himself. In 1495 he printed also an advertisement of the *Nuremberg Chronicles*.[1]

Though Spire was not an important town in the history of printing, a book was printed there as early as 1471. This was the *Postilla super Apocalypsin* [Hain, 13,310]. It is a quarto, printed in a rude

[1] These early book catalogues supply a very great deal of curious information, and are very well worth careful study. An extremely good article by Wilhelm Meyer, containing reprints of twenty-two, was issued some years ago in the *Centralblatt für Bibliothekswesen;* and since that time reprints of a few others have appeared in the same magazine.

Roman type, but with a Gothic V. Two other works of Augustine and one of Huss (*Gesta Christi*) are known, printed in a larger type, but without date, place, or name of printer. It has usually been assumed, on what grounds is not stated, that these books were printed by Peter Drach; but as at present no book is known in this type with his name, it is perhaps wiser to assign them to an unknown printer. Peter Drach's first dated book was issued in 1477, and the history of his press at this time is particularly interesting. The type in which his *Vocabularius utriusque Juris* of May 1477 is printed, is absolutely the same as that used in December of the same year for printing the *Vocabularius ex quo*, printed, according to its colophon, by Nicholas Bechtermuntze at Eltvil. On this subject it is best to quote Mr. Hessels' own words, for to him this discovery is due:[1]—

'I may here observe that Type 3 [that of Bechtermüncze in 1477] is exactly the same as that used by Peter Drach at Spire. When I received this *Vocabulary* [*ex quo* of 1477] from Munich, the only book I had seen of Drach was the *Leonardi de Utino Sermones*, published in 1479; and it occurred to me that Bechtermuncze had probably ceased to print about this time, and might have transferred his type to Drach. But this appears not to have been the case, as Drach published already, on the 18th May 1477, the *Vocabularius Juris utriusque*, printed with the

[1] *Gutenberg; Was he the Inventor of Printing?* By J. H. Hessels. ondon, 1882. 8vo. P. 181.

very same type, and must therefore have been in possession of his type simultancously with Bechtermuncze. The question therefore arises, Did Drach perhaps print the 1477 *Vocabulary* for Nicolaus Bechtermuncze ?'

This question must, unfortunately, be left for the present where Mr. Hessels has left it, but it offers a most interesting point for further research.

From 1477, Peter Drach continued to print at any rate to the end of the fifteenth century; but it is perhaps possible that there were a father and son of the same name, whose various books have not been separated. The *Omeliarum opus* of 1482 [Hain, 8789] is spoken of as 'factore Petro Drach juniore in inclita Spirensium urbe impressum.' The only other interesting printers at Spire were the brothers John and Conrad Hijst, whose names are found in the preface to an edition of the *Philobiblon* of Richard de Bury, which they printed about 1483. They used an ornamental Gothic type, generally confused with that belonging to Reyser of Eichstadt, and their unsigned books are almost always described by Hain and others as printed 'typis Reyserianis.'

Only one printer is known to have been at Esslingen in the fifteenth century. This was Conrad Fyner, who began to print in 1472, and continued in the town till 1480. Though the first dated book is 1472, it is most probable that several of the undated books should be placed earlier. Fyner's first small type is extremely like one used at Strasburg by Eggestein, if indeed it is not identical, and their books are constantly confused. In 1473, Fyner printed Gerson's *Collectorium super Magnificat*, the first book containing printed musical notes; and in 1475, *P. Niger contra perfidos Judeos*, which contains the first specimen of Hebrew type. One book in Fyner's type [Hain, *9335] is said to be printed by Johannes Hug de Goppingen. In 1481, Fyner moved to Urach, where he printed one book, and after that date he disappears.

At Lavingen only one book is known to have been printed in the fifteenth century. It is the *Augustinus de consensu evangelistarum* [Hain, *1981], issued on April 12, 1473. Madden conjectures from the appearance of the type and the capital letters that the book was printed by John Zainer of Ulm. Both type and capitals, however, are different, but their resemblance is quite natural considering the short distance between Ulm and Lavingen.

At an early period Ulm was very important as a centre for wood engraving, and several block-books are known to have been produced there. An edition of the *Ars Moriendi* is signed Ludwig ze Ulm, whom Dr. Hassler conjectures to have been Ludwig Hohenwang. The earliest printer that we find mentioned in a dated book is John Zainer of Reutlingen, no doubt a relation of Gunther Zainer the printer at Augsburg. He issued in 1473 a work by Boccaccio, *De præclaris mulieribus*, illustrated with a number of woodcuts, and having also woodcut initials and borders. He printed from this time to the end of the century, many of his books being ornamented. Another printer at Ulm to be noticed is Conrad Dinckmut, who printed from 1482 to 1496. He was probably a wood engraver, for he illustrated many of his books with woodcuts, and also produced a xylographic *Donatus*, of which there is an imperfect copy in the Bodleian.

·In 1473, printing was introduced into Merseburg by Luke Brandis, who moved in 1475 to Lubeck. In 1475, also, Conrad Elyas began to print at Breslau, and by 1480 no fewer than twenty-three towns had printing presses. Between 1480 and 1490 the art was introduced into fifteen more towns, and between 1490 and 1501 into twelve. So that the total number of places in Germany where printing was practised in the fifteenth century is fifty.

Basle was the first city of Switzerland into which printing was introduced, but it is hard to determine when this took place. The earliest printer was Berthold Rodt, or Ruppel of Hanau, who is supposed to be the same man as the Bertholdus of Hanau who figures in the lawsuit of 1455 as a servant of Gutenberg. It is not till 1473, in the colophon of the *Repertorium Vocabulorum* of Conrad de Mure, that we find either his name or a date ; but many books are known printed in the same type. One of these, the *Moralia in Job* of St. Gregory, was printed in or before 1468, for one copy contains a manuscript note showing that it was bought in that year by

Joseph de Vergers, an ecclesiastic of Mainz. About 1474, Berthold began to print a Bible, but finished only the first volume, dying, it is supposed, about that time. The second volume was printed by Bernard Richel, and is dated 1475. The most important printers of Basle were Wenssler, Amorbach, and Froben. About 1469, Helyas de Louffen, a canon of the Abbey of Berǫmunster, began to print, and in 1470 issued the *Mammotrectus* of Marchesinus, finished on the Vigil of St. Martin, the exact day and year in which Schœffer finished his edition of the same book. Bernard says that the two editions are certainly different, and could not have been copied one from the other, so that the similarity of date must be looked upon as a curious coincidence. This *Mammotrectus* is the first dated book issued in Switzerland, and is printed in the most remarkable Gothic type used anywhere in the fifteenth century. Many of the capital letters if found by themselves could not be read, and it is a type which once seen can never be forgotten. At the foot of each column in the book is a letter which looks like a signature, but which is put there for the purpose of a number to the column. Helyas de Louffen died in 1475, having printed about eight books, some in Gothic and some in Roman type.

Before the end of the fifteenth century printing presses were at work in five other towns of Switzerland : Geneva (1478), Promentour (1482), Lausanne (1493), Trogen (1497), and Sursee (1500).

CHAPTER IV.

ITALY.

ITALIAN historians have several times attempted to bring forward Pamphilò Castaldi as the inventor of printing. It is little use to recapitulate here the various unsupported assertions on which this claim is based,—a claim which, if it ever had, has now ceased to have any sensible supporters.

We may safely assume, with our present knowledge, that the art of printing was introduced into Italy in 1465 by two Germans, Conrad Sweynheym and Arnold Pannartz. On their arrival in Italy they settled first in the Monastery of Saint Scholastica at Subiaco, an establishment of Benedictines, of which Cardinal Turrecremata was Abbot, where they would be in congenial society, since, as Cardinal Quirini says, many of the inmates were Germans.

The first book which they printed was a *Donatus pro puerulis*, of which they said in their list, printed in 1472, 'unde imprimendi initium sumpsimus.' Unfortunately, of this *Donatus* no copy is known, though rumours of a copy in a private collection in Italy have from time to time been circulated. The earliest book from their press of which copies are in existence, is the Cicero *De Oratore*, printed before 30th September 1465.[1] It has been always a moot point whether this Cicero *De Oratore* or the Mainz *Ciceronis Officia et Paradoxa*, printed in the same year, can justly claim to be the first printed Latin classic, while the claims of the *De Officiis* of Zel, which, though undated, is very probably as early, have been entirely ignored.

The Subiaco *De Oratore* is a large quarto of 109 leaves, with thirty lines to the page. Like the first German books, it is beautifully printed, and shows few signs of being an early production. Sweynheym and Pannartz must have learnt their business carefully, for this their first book is printed by half sheets, *i.e.* two pages at a time, though other printers were still printing their quartos page by page.

On the 29th October 1465 these printers issued their first dated book, the first edition of Lactantius *De divinis institutionibus*. Of this book 275 copies were printed. It is a small folio of 188 leaves, and thirty-six lines to the page, printed in a type which, though Roman, is very Gothic in appearance, and is sometimes called semi-Gothic. The smaller letters have a curious resemblance to those used by Zainer

---

[1] This book has usually been dated later than the *Lactantius*, that is, after 29th October 1465; but M. Fumagalli, in his *Dei primi libri a stampa in Italia*, Lugano, 1875, 8vo, describes a copy containing a manuscript note dated 'Pridie Kal. Octobres, M.cccc.lxv.,' so that the *Cicero* must be considered the first known book printed in Italy. On the other hand, it should be noticed that some authorities consider the inscription to be a forgery.

at Ulm and by Schussler at Augsburg in their earliest books, though the capital letters are quite different.

The fourth and last book printed by Sweynheym and Pannartz at Subiaco was an edition of the *De civitate dei* of Saint Augustine. This is a large folio of 270 leaves, with two columns, and forty-four lines to the page. It was issued on the 12th June 1467 ; and though it contains no name of either printer or place, can be easily identified by the type. A copy in the Bibliothèque Nationale has an extremely interesting manuscript note, which tells us that Leonardus Dathus, 'Episcopus Massanus,' bought the book from the Germans themselves, living at Rome, who were producing innumerable books of that sort by means of printing, not writing, in November 1467. This note is valuable in two ways ; it puts it beyond doubt who the printers of the book were, and it also enables us to determine more precisely the date when they left Subiaco. The *Augustine* was finished in June, and by November the printers were at Rome. As they issued a book in Rome in 1467, and would take some time to settle in their new establishment and prepare their new types, we may take it as probable that they left the Monastery of Subiaco as soon as possible after the printing of the *Augustine*.

About June, then, Sweynheym and Pannartz left the Monastery of Subiaco and transferred their printing materials to Rome, finding a home in a house

belonging to the brothers Peter and Francis de
Maximis. The semi-Gothic fount of type which had
been used at Subiaco was discarded in favour of one
more Roman in character, though heavily cut and
not so graceful as the Venetian of the same period.
A curious appearance is given to it by the invariable
use of the long f. Their first venture was again a
work of Cicero, the *Epistolæ ad familiares*, a large
quarto of thirty-one lines to the page. It has the
following colophon :—

> ' Hoc Conradus opus Suueynheym ordine miro
> Arnoldusque simul pannarts una aede colendi
> Gente theotonica : romæ expediere sodales.
> In domo Petri de Maximo. M.CCCC.LXVII.'

From this time forward, under the able supervision of the Bishop of Aleria, Sweynheym and
Pannartz continued to print with the greatest industry, but they did not meet with the support which
they merited. In 1472 they had become so badly off
that a letter was written to Pope Sixtus IV. pointing
out their distress, and asking for assistance. This
letter, printed on one sheet, is usually found in the
fifth volume of Nicholas de Lyra's *Commentary
on the Bible*, printed in 1472. Its great bibliographical interest lies in the fact that the printers
gave a list of what they had printed and the number
of copies they issued. In the list twenty-eight works
are mentioned, and the number of volumes amounted
altogether to 11,475. They usually issued 275 copies
of each work which they printed.

This list also clearly shows the extraordinary
influence of the new learning so actively promoted
by Cosmo de Medici and encouraged by his grandson
Lorenzo. The majority of the books in this list
are classics, either in their original Latin or in Latin
translations from the Greek; and that the printers
were anxious to benefit scholars, is shown by the
assertion of the Bishop of Aleria in the prefatory
letter to the *Ciceronis Epistolæ ad Atticum* of 1470,
where it is said that they had produced their editions
of Cicero at the lowest possible price, "ad pauperum
commoditatem."

To judge from the results, the appeal to the Pope
was of little effect, for in 1473 Conrad Sweynheym
gave up the business of printing, and confined his
attention to engraving on metal; while Pannartz continued to print by himself up till the end of 1476,
issuing in those three years about twelve books. The
last book on which Pannartz was engaged was a
new edition of the *Letters of St. Jerome*, but he only
finished one volume. Three years later, George
Laver, who seems to have acquired the type, issued
the second volume. It is therefore quite probable, as
is generally asserted, that Pannartz died in 1476 or
early in 1477. Sweynheym, ever since he had given
up printing, had been engaged in engraving a series
of maps to illustrate Ptolemy's *Geography;* but, after
working three years upon them, died before they
were finished. The edition of Ptolemy was finally
issued in 1478 by Arnold Buckinck, a German, who

in his preface said that he was anxious 'that the emendations of Calderinus—who also died before the book was printed—and the results of Sweynheym's most ingenious mechanical contrivances might not be lost to the learned world.'

'Magister vero Conradus Sweynheym, Germanus, a quo formandorum Romæ librorum ars primum profecta est, occasione hinc sumpta posteritati consulens animum primum ad hanc doctrinam capescendam applicuit. Subinde mathematicis adhibitis viris quemadmodum tabulis eneis imprimerentur edocuit, triennioque in hac cura consumpto diem obiit. In cujus vigilarum laborumque partem non inferiori ingenio ac studio Arnoldus Buckinck e Germania vir apprime eruditus ad imperfectum opus succedens, ne Domitii Conradique obitu eorum vigiliæ emendationesque sine testimonio perirent neve virorum eruditorum censuram fugerent immensæ subtilitatis machinimenta, examussim ad unum perfecit.'

The book contains twenty-seven maps, each map being printed on two separate leaves facing each other, and printed only on one side. The letters which occur on the maps in the names of places are evidently punched from single dies, and not cut on the plate, as would have been expected. The letterpress of the book is not printed in any type used by Sweynheym or Pannartz, which shows that Buckinck was the absolute printer of the book.

Ulric Hahn, who contests with Sweynheym and Pannartz for the honour of having introduced printing into Rome, issued as his first book, in 1467, the *Meditations* of Cardinal Torquemada, better known perhaps as Turrecremata. It is illustrated with thirty-three woodcuts of inferior execution, and is printed in a large Gothic type. This type the printer discarded the following year for one of Roman letter ; but odd types from the Gothic fount frequently make their appearance among the Roman, and serve as a means of distinguishing Hahn's books from others in similar Roman type. As a case in point, we may mention the early and probably first edition of *Catullus*, wrongly ascribed to Andrea Belfortis of Ferrara and other printers. This book is in Hahn's Roman type, and contains three capital letters from his Gothic fount,—a more sure means of identification than a fancied allusion to a printer's name.[1] For a short time, from 1470 to 1472, Hahn's books were edited by Campanus, a scholar of such fame and erudition, that the printer was able to rival Sweynheym and Pannartz, with their editor the Bishop of Aleria ; but on Campanus taking his departure for Ratisbon, the prestige of Hahn's press declined. From the pen of Campanus came perhaps the punning colophons which play upon the name of Hahn, in Latin, Gallus,

---

[1] The edition of *Catullus*, mentioned above, is ascribed to Andrea Belfortis, because the words 'cui Francia nomen' occur in the prefatory verses ; and the same words occur, referring to Belfortis, in a book printed by him. But the types of the *Catullus* and those used by Andrea Belfortis are certainly different, while both the types of the *Catullus* are found in other books printed by Hahn. The *Catullus* has also a Registrum Chartarum, which was almost invariably put to his books by Hahn.

E

meaning in English a cock. Upon the departure of Campanus, Hahn took in partnership one Simon Nicolai Chardella of Lucca, who seems to have supplied the money as well as superintended the publishing, and they continued to work together till 1474. From this date till 1478, Hahn continued to work alone, ending in that year as he had begun, with an edition of the *Meditationes* of Torquemada. His former partner, Simon Nicolai, started a press on his own account, having as an associate his cousin.

The latest writer[1] on the early history of printing in Venice has again revived the question as to the correctness of the date of the *Decor Puellarum*. Though he still clings to the possibility of the date 1461 being trustworthy, the weight of evidence, all of which is carefully stated, is decisively in favour of its being a misprint for 1471.

It would be useless to recapitulate here all the arguments in favour of Jenson having printed in 1461, when it is now generally admitted that John of Spire was the first printer at Venice, and that his first book was the *Epistolæ familiares* of Cicero, issued in 1469. Of this book only one hundred copies were printed. On the 18th September 1469, the Collegio of Venice granted to John of Spire a monopoly of printing in that district for five years; and this document distinctly indicates that he was

---

[1] *The Venetian Printing Press.* By Horatio F. Brown. London, 1891. 4to.

the first printer at Venice. He did not, however, live to obtain the advantage of this privilege, 'nullius est vigoris quia obiit magister et auctor,' says a contemporary marginal note to the record, for he died in 1470. Previous to his death he printed a *Pliny*, the first volume of a *Livy*, two editions of the *Epistolæ ad familiares*, and part of the Augustine *De civitate dei*, which was finished by his brother Windelin.

> 'Subita sed morte peremptus
> Non potuit cœptum Venetis finire volumen.'

Windelin of Spire was a very prolific printer, and continued to issue books without intermission from the time of his brother's death, in 1470, to his own in 1478. But among the early Venetian printers the most important was certainly Nicholas Jenson. A Frenchman by birth, he passed his apprenticeship in the Paris Mint, and became afterwards the head of the Mint at Tours. In 1458, in consequence of the stories of the invention of printing, he was sent by Charles VII. to Mainz to learn the art, and introduce it into France. Jenson returned in 1461, when Louis XI. had just been crowned ; but he does not seem to have settled in France, and we first hear of him again in 1470 as a printer at Venice. From 1470 to 1480 he printed continuously, issuing, according to Sardini, at least one hundred and fifty-five editions, though this number must be considerably under the mark. His will was drawn up on the 7th September 1480, and he died in the same

month. The fame of Jenson rests on the extraordinary beauty of his Roman type, of which he had
but one fount, and which, though frequently copied,
was never equalled. In 1474 he began to use Gothic
type, owing to its great saving of space ; and in 1471,
in the *Epistolæ familiares*, he used Greek type in
the quotations, the first instance of its employment
in Venice. It is curious that, with its devotion to
the new learning, Venice should not have been the
first to issue a Greek book. Jenson had frequently
to use Greek type in his books, but he never printed
a complete work in that language. Milan led the
way, printing the *Greek Grammar* of Lascaris in 1476;
and it was not till 1485 that Venice issued its first
Greek book, the *Erotemata* of Chrysoloras.

In 1470, another German, Christopher Valdarfer of
Ratisbon, began to print. He left Venice in 1473,
and settled at Milan, and the books which he printed
at the former place are very rare and few in number.
The best known is the *Decameron* of 1471, the first
edition of the book, familiar to all readers of Dibdin.

In 1471 was issued the *De medicinis universalibus*,
printed by Clemens Sacerdos (Clement of Padua),
the first Italian printer in Venice ; and in the year
following, Philippus Petri,[1] the first native Venetian
printer, began to print.

Between 1470 and 1480 at least fifty printers were

---

[1] This printer's name seems to have led to a certain amount of
confusion. He was Filippo the son of Piero, in Latin, Philippus
Petri ; but after his father's death, about the end of 1477, he calls
himself Philippus quondam Petri, Filippo son of the late Piero.

at work in Venice, and among the most important were John de Colonia, John Manthen de Gerretzem, Erhard Ratdolt, Octavianus Scotus. Erhard Ratdolt is especially of importance, for he was practically the first to introduce wood engravings in his books. In 1476, Ratdolt and his partners, Peter Loeslein and Bernard Pictor, began their work together by issuing a *Calendar* of Regiomontanus, with a very beautiful title-page surrounded by a woodcut border. From that time onwards, woodcuts were used in many Venetian books; and at last, in 1499, there appeared there that unsurpassed illustrated book the *Hypnerotomachia* of Franciscus Columna.

The history of the later Venetian press during the last ten years of the fifteenth century would require at least a volume. So far as the history of typography itself is concerned, there is nothing of interest to be noticed; but in the general history of printing Venice holds the highest place, for more printers printed there than in any other city of Europe. Of course, amongst this endless outpour of the press many important books were issued, but there are few which have any interest for the historian of printing.

There is, however, one printer who must always make this period celebrated. Aldus Manutius was born at Bassiano in 1450, and began to print at Venice in 1494. His main idea when he commenced to work was to print Greek books; and it was perhaps for that reason that he settled in Venice, where so many manuscripts were preserved, and where so many Greeks resided. His first two books, both issued in 1494, are the *Galeomyomachia* and the *De Herone et Leandro* of Musæus. In 1496 he obtained a copyright for twenty years in such Greek books as he might print, and from this time forward a large number were issued as fast as possible. So great was the hurry, that the editors in some cases did not scruple to hand over to the compositors the original manuscripts themselves from which the edition was taken, with their own emendations and corrections scribbled upon them. But this custom was not confined to the Aldine press, for Martin[1] tells us that the Codex Ravennas of Aristophanes was actually used by the compositors as the working copy from which part of the Giunta edition of 1515 was set up.

In 1499, Aldus married the daughter of Andrea de Torresani, himself a great printer, and in 1500 founded the Aldine Academy, the home of so many editors, and the source of so many scholarly editions of the sixteenth century. The end of the fifteenth century saw, at any rate, two rivals in Greek printing to Aldus: Gabriel da Brasichella, who with his associates published in 1498 the *Epistles of Phalaris* and *Æsop's Fables;* and, in 1499, Zaccharia Caliergi of Crete, who printed with others or alone up till 1509. Caliergi, it would appear, was hardly a rival of Aldus; they were, at any rate, so far friendly that Aldus sold Caliergi's editions along with his own.

[1] Martin, *Les scholies du Manuscrit d'Aristophane à Ravenna.*

In 1470 a press was set up at Foligno, in the house of Emilianus de Orsinis, by John Numeister, a native of Mainz, who is generally said to have been an associate and pupil of Gutenberg. This story seems to be founded upon an assertion put forward by Fischer, that a copy of the *Tractatus de celebratione missarum*, in the University Library at Mainz, contains a rubric stating that the book was printed by Gutenberg and Numeister in 1463. If this note ever existed, which is very doubtful, it is clearly a forgery, for the book in which it is said to occur was not printed till about 1480.

The first book in which we find Numeister's name is the *De bello Italico contra Gothos*, by Aretinus, printed in 1470; and about the same date he printed an edition of the *Epistolæ familiares* of Cicero. In 1472 appeared the first edition of *Dante;* between that year and 1479 we hear nothing of Numeister. In 1479 an edition of the *Meditationes* of Turrecremata appeared with his name, printed in a large church type, not unlike, though not, as is often said, the same as, the type of the forty-two line Bible, and containing very fine engraved cuts. This book is generally stated, for some unknown reason, to have been printed at Mainz. After this date we find no further mention of Numeister; but M. Claudin[1] has written a monograph to show that he was the printer of the edition of the *Meditationes* of Turrecremata issued at Albi in 1481, a book remarkable for its

---

[1] *Origine de l'Imprimerie à Albi et en Languedoc.*

wonderful engravings on metal, and of the *Missale
Lugdunense*, printed at Lyons in 1487, which is stated
in the colophon to have been printed by 'Magistrum
Jo. alemanum de magontia impressorem.'

After 1470 the spread of printing in Italy was very
rapid. In 1471 we find it beginning at Bologna,
Ferrara, Florence, Milan, Naples, Pavia, and Treviso.

The first complete edition of *Ovid* was produced in
1471, and is the first book printed at Bologna, the
printer being Balthasar Azzoguidi, 'primus in sua
civitate artis impressoriæ inventor,' as he calls himself in the preface to the book. Andrea Portilia
must also have been amongst the earliest printers at
Bologna, though his only dated book is 1473, for in
that year he returned to Parma. Among the many
printers who worked in the town, none are better
known, from the frequency with which their names
occur in colophons, than the various members of
the family 'de Benedictis,' who worked from 1488
onwards.

Andreas Belfortis, a Frenchman, was the first to
print at Ferrara, issuing in 1471 at least three books,
of which the earliest, published in July, is an edition
of *Martial* (which has catchwords to the quires in
the latter portion). This was followed by editions of
Poggio and *Augustinus Dathus*. Belfortis continued
to print till 1493. A certain Augustinus Carner, who
printed a few books between 1474 and 1476, printed
in 1475 the rare *Teseide* of Boccaccio, the first printed
poem in the Italian language. De Rossi, in his

tract, *De typographia Ebræo-Ferrariensi*, gives a long description of some Hebrew books printed at Ferrara in 1477, which must be the first printed in that language, though some words are found in a book printed at Esslingen in 1475.

The first printer at Milan was Anthony Zarotus, and his earliest book, with both name and date, is the *Virgil* of 1472. In the previous year, four books had been issued without any printer's name, but the identity of the type with that of the *Virgil* shows Zarotus to have printed these also. Mention has often been made of a certain *Terence*, printed in 1470, March 13. It is quoted by Hain (15,371), who had not seen it, and by Panzer (ii. 11. 2), and a copy was said to be in the library of the Earl of Pembroke, the home of many mysterious books. It is often quoted as the first book with signatures. It was doubtless a copy of the edition of March 13, 1481, in which some ingenious person had erased the last two figures, xi, of the date. It is very probable that there was at first some connection between Zarotus and Philip de Lavagna ; and it was perhaps at the latter's expense, and through his means, that Zarotus first printed. Certainly, in the colophon of a book printed in 1473, probably by Christopher Valdarfer, are the words 'per Philippum de Lavagnia, hujus artis stampandi in hac urbe primum latorem atque inventorem ;' but it is quite possible that the words should not be taken in too narrow a sense, and that Philip de Lavagna simply means to speak of himself as the first person to introduce printing into Milan, not as printer, but as patron.

The history of the first printers in this town is very interesting, for they entered into various partnerships, and the documents relating to these have been preserved and published,[1] throwing a good deal of light on some of the customs and methods of the early printers. In 1476 was printed at Milan the *Grammar* of Constantine Lascaris, the first book printed in Greek; and in 1481, a Greek version of the *Psalms*, the first portion of the Bible printed in this language.

At Florence, Bernard Cennini, the celebrated goldsmith and assistant of Ghiberti, printed, with the assistance of two of his sons, an edition of the Commentary of Servius on Virgil. It was begun towards the end of 1471, and not finished till October 1472, but is the first book printed at Florence. This is the only book known to have been printed by Cennini; but it is not unlikely that in his capacity of goldsmith he did work for other printers in cutting type. The most interesting press at Florence in the fifteenth century, was that founded in the Monastery of St. James of Ripoli by Dominic de Pistoia, the head of the establishment. Beginning with a *Donatus*, of which every copy has disappeared, it was carried on briskly up till the time of his death in 1484, issuing, according to Hain, just over fifty works; according to De Rossi, nearly one hundred. The account books

[1] Saxius, *Bibliotheca scriptorum Mediolanensium.* Milan, 1745. Fol.

connected with this press have been preserved, and from them we can learn the price of the various articles used by the printers, such as paper, ink, type-metal. Several kinds of paper are mentioned, and identified, as a rule, by their watermarks. We have paper from Fabriano with the mark of a crossbow, a different paper from the same place marked with a cross, and two sorts of paper from Pescia marked with spectacles and a glove. There are several celebrated books printed at Florence before 1500 which cannot be passed over. In 1477 was issued the *Monte Santo di Dio*, said to contain the first copperplate engraving ; and in 1481, the celebrated *Dante*, with engravings by Baccio Baldini after the designs of Botticelli. Most copies of this book contain only a few of the plates, while about eight copies are known with the full number. Some celebrated Greek books also were issued at Florence, notably in 1488 the first edition of *Homer* printed by Demetrius Chalcondylas at the expense of two brothers, Bernardus and Nerius Nerlii. There is a copy of this book in the British Museum, which was bought by Mr. Barnard, librarian to George III., for seven shillings. One complete copy on vellum is known, in the library of St. Mark's at Venice.

Towards the end of the fifteenth century, Francis de Alopa printed five Greek books entirely in capital letters, the *Anthologia* of 1494, *Callimachus*, *Euripides* (four plays only), *Apollonius Rhodius*, 1496, *Poetae Gnomici*, and *Musæus*. It is very probable that the

'editio princeps' of *Lucian*, which was printed at
Florence, but is ascribed by Ebert to Caliergi at
Venice, was also printed at this press.

Under the patronage of Ferdinand I., King of
Naples, Sixtus Riessinger of Strasburg began to
print there in 1471, and continued till 1479. He
seems to have been in high favour with the king, who
offered him a bishopric, which was, however, refused.
In 1472, Arnaldus de Bruxella set up his press, using
(unlike most other printers) Roman type only. The
large M and small *y* are of a curious form and easily
recognisable, while the final *us* in words is always
represented by an abbreviation. Most of the books
printed by him are rare ; of the *Horace* and *Petrarch*,
only single copies are known ; and it was for the sake
of acquiring these two books, so Dibdin tells us, that
Lord Spencer bought the Cassano Library. Hain
mentions seventeen books printed by this Arnaldus
de Bruxella, and out of that number he had seen only
one. Van der Meersch gives twenty-three ; but some
are doubtful.

Pavia is more celebrated for the number of books
it produced than for their interest, and it is only
mentioned here as one of the towns to which printing
is said to have been introduced in 1471.

The last town to be mentioned in this group is
Treviso, where, in 1471, that wandering printer
Gerardus de Lisa began to print. In his first year he
printed several books, but his industry gradually got
less. In 1477 we find him at Venice, in 1480 at

Cividad di Friuli (Civitas Austriæ), and in 1484 at Udina.

1472 saw printing established in Cremona, Mantua, Monreale, Padua, Parma, and Verona, and from this time onwards it spread rapidly over the whole of Italy, being introduced into seventy-one towns before the end of the fifteenth century. For the study of typography the Italian-presses are not nearly so interesting as those of other countries, but from a literary point of view they are immeasurably superior. The Renaissance movement had been at work in Italy during the whole of the fifteenth century, and the great impetus given by the fall of Constantinople was acting most powerfully when the printing press was introduced. Italy was then the sole guardian of the ancient civilisation, and was prepared for a more rapid method of reproducing its early treasures and spreading the learning of its newer scholars.

CHAPTER V.

FRANCE.

A CURIOUS prelude has been discovered within the last few years to the history of the introduction of printing into France. L'Abbé Requin, searching through the archives of Avignon, brought to light a series of entries relating to printing, 'ars scribendi artificialiter,' as it is there called, dated as far back as the year 1444.[1]

The information obtained from the notarial books, fairly complete in its way, is as follows :—A certain silversmith, named Procopius Waldfoghel of Prague, was settled at Avignon by the beginning of 1444, and was working at printing, in conjunction with a student of the university, Manaudus Vitalis, whom he had supplied with printing materials.

In a notarial act of the 4th July of that year, the following materials are mentioned :—'Duo abecedaria calibis et duas formas ferreas, unum instrumentum calibis vocatum vitis, quadraginta octo formas stangni necnon diversas alias formas ad artem scri-

[1] *L'Imprimerie à Avignon en* 1444. By L'Abbé Requin. Paris, 1890. *Origines de l'Imprimerie en France* (Avignon, 1444). By L'Abbé Requin. Paris, 1891. *Les Origines de l'Imprimerie à Avignon.* Par M. Duhamel. 1890.

bendi pertinentes.' Waldfoghel was evidently the maker of the materials and the teacher of the art, and he seems to have supplied his apprentices with such tools as would enable them to print for themselves.

In 1444, besides Manaudus Vitalis, Waldfoghel had as apprentices, Girardus Ferrose of Treves, Georgius de la Jardina, Arnaldus de Cosselhac, and a Jew named Davinus de Cadarossia.

From a document dated 10th March 1446, we learn that Waldfoghel, having two years previously taught the art of printing to the Jew, had promised to cut for him a set of twenty-seven Hebrew letters and to give him certain other materials. In return for this, the Jew was to teach him to dye in a particular way all kinds of textile material, and to keep secret all he learnt on the art of printing.

In another document, of 5th April 1446, relating to the partnership of Waldfoghel, Manaudus Vitalis, and Arnaldus de Cosselhac, and the selling of his share to the remaining two by Vitalis, we have mention made of 'nonnulla instrumenta sive artificia causa artificialiter scribendi, tam de ferro, de callibe, de cupro, de lethono, de plumbo, de stagno et de fuste.'

There seems to be no doubt that these various entries refer to printing with movable types; they cannot refer to xylographic printing, nor to stencilling. At the same time, there is no evidence to point to any particular kind of printing; and the various materials mentioned would rather make it appear that the Avignon invention was some method of stamping letters or words from cut type, than printing from cast type in a press. Until some specimen is found of this Avignon work, from which some definite knowledge can be obtained, the question must be left undecided, for it is useless to try to extract from words capable of various renderings any exact meaning. Our information at present is only sufficient to enable us to say that some kind of printing was being practised at Avignon as early as 1444. It seems, too, impossible that, had this invention been printing of the ordinary kind, nothing more should have come of the experiment; and we know of no printing in France before 1470.

Les neuf Preux, the only block-book executed in France, has been already noticed. It is considered to have been printed at Paris about 1455.

The first printing press was naturally started at Paris, the great centre of learning and culture, and it seems strange that so important an invention should not have been introduced earlier than 1470. Many specimens of the art had been seen, for Fust in 1466 and Schœffer in 1468 had visited the capital to sell their books. If we may believe the manuscript preserved in the library of the Arsenal, the French King, in October 1458, sent out Nicholas Jenson to learn the art; but he, 'on his return to France, finding Charles VII. dead, set up his establishment elsewhere.' Probably a strong antagonism to the new art would be shown by the immense number of professional copyists and scribes who gained their livelihood in connection with the university, though the demand for manuscripts continued in France for some time after the introduction of printing. Many of the wealthy, moreover, refused to recognise the innovation, and admitted no printed book into their libraries, so that the scribes were not at once deprived of employment. Many of these men who had been employed in producing manuscripts, soon turned to the new art as a means of employment, becoming themselves printers, or assisting in the production of books, as rubricators or illuminators.

In 1470, thanks to the exertions of Jean Heynlyn and Guillaume Fichet, both men of high position in the University of Paris, a printing press was set up in the precincts of the Sorbonne by three Germans, Martin Crantz, Ulrich Gering of Constance, and Michael Friburger of Colmar. The first book they issued was *Gasparini Pergamensis Epistolarum Opus,* a quarto of 118 leaves, with a prefatory letter to Heynlyn, which fixes the date of its production in 1470, and an interesting colophon—

> ' Ut sol lumen, sic doctrinam fundis in orbem,
>   Musarum nutrix, regia Parisius.
> Hinc prope divinam, tu, quam Germania novit,
>   Artem scribendi suscipe promerita.
> Primos ecce libros quos hæc industria finxit
>   Francorum in terris, ædibus atque tuis.
> Michael, Udalricus Martinusque magistri
>   Hos impresserunt ac facient alios.'

The classical taste of the patrons of the first press

is strongly shown by its productions, for within the first three years a most important series of classical books had been published. *Florus* and *Sallust* (both first editions), *Terence*, Virgil's *Eclogues* and *Georgics*, *Juvenal* and *Persius*, Cicero's *Tusculan Disputations*, and *Valerius Maximus*, are amongst the books they issued.

In 1470–71 these printers finished thirteen books, while in the following year, before moving from the Sorbonne, they printed no less than seventeen. Some time towards the end of 1472 they left the Sorbonne and migrated to the Rue St. Jacques, where two other printers—Kaiser and Stoll—were already settled in partnership at the sign of the Green Ball (Intersignium viridis follis).

In 1472 was issued the *Gasparini Orthographia*. The copy of this book in the library at Basle contains a unique supplementary letter from Fichet to Robert Gaguin, in which is the following interesting statement about the invention of printing :—
'Report says that there (in Germany), not far from the city of Mainz (Ferunt enim illic, haud procul a civitate Maguncia), there was a certain John, whose surname was Gutenberg, who first of any thought out the art of printing . . . by which art books are printed from metal letters.'[1]

---

[1] Mr. Hessels, in his *Haarlem the Birthplace of Printing, not Mentz*, attempts to weaken the value of this evidence, and translates 'ferunt enim illic' as 'a rumour current in Germany,'—a striking example of ingenious mistranslation. 'Illic' is, of course, to be taken with what follows, and is further defined by 'haud procul a civitate Maguncia.'

Gafpatini pergamenfis clariffimi orato/
tif/epiftolaꝶ liber foeliciter incipit;

Audeo plurimum ac lætor in
ea te fententia effe/ut nihil a
me fieri fine caufa putef·Ego
enĩ etfi multoꝶ uerebar fufpi
tionef/ꝗ a me fempronĩũ antiquũ fami//
liarẽ meũ reiiciebã-tamẽ cũ ad incredibi/
lẽ animi tui fapiẽtiã iudiciũ meũ refere//
bã! nihil erat q̃re id a te improbari pu/
tarem·Nam cum & meof noffef moref!&
illius naturã ñ ignotares!ñ dubitabã qd
de hoc facto meo iudicaturus effes· Non
igĩt haf ad te fcribo lrãf/quo nouam tibi
de rebuf a me geftif opinionem faciã?fed
ut fi quando aliter homĩef noftrof de me
fẽtire intelligcs! tu ꝗ probe caufam meã
nofti/defenfionẽ meã fufcipiaf·Hæc fi fe/
ceris! nihil eft quo ulterius officium tu/
um requiram·Valc ;

Between the two printing offices in the Rue St. Jacques a keen spirit of rivalry arose ; and this was carried to such an extent, that no sooner was a book printed by one than another edition was issued by the other,—a sign that the demand for such books must have been large. The earliest type used by these first printers is an exquisite Roman, the letters being more square than the best Roman type of Venice, and far surpassing it in beauty. Round brackets are used, and all the generally used stops are found. The first type of Kaiser and Stoll is also Roman, with neat and very distinctive capitals, and the small *l* has a short stroke coming out on the left side about half-way up, a peculiarity still retained in all the Roman type belonging to the ' Imprimerie Nationale.' The popular taste seems to have been for Gothic type, and very few printers made use of Roman before the year 1500.

About 1478, Gering's two partners, Crantz and Friburger, left him ; but he himself continued to print on for many years. About this date, too, the character of the books issued from the Paris presses began entirely to change. In 1477, Pasquier Bon-homme had issued the first French book printed in that city, the *Grandes Chroniques de France*, and from this time forward classical books were neglected, and nothing printed but romances and chronicles, service-books and grammars, and such books as were in popular demand. During the twelve or fourteen years after the first French book appeared, not one

classical book a year was issued; and it was not till
1495, the year of Charles VIII.'s return from Italy,
that the printing of classical books began to revive
and increase.

In 1485, Antoine Verard, the most important figure
in the early history of Parisian printing, begins his
career with an edition of the *Decameron*. He was,
however, more of a publisher than a printer, the
majority of the books which contain his name having
been printed for him by other printers. From his
establishment came numberless editions of chronicles
and romances, some copies of which were printed on
vellum and illuminated. A very fine series of such
books is now in the British Museum; these were
originally bought by Henry VII., and formed part of
the old Royal Library.

Among the more important printers who printed
before 1490 should be mentioned Guy Marchant,
Jean du Pré, Guillaume le Fèvre, Antoine Cayllaut,
Pierre Levet, Pierre le Rouge, and Jean Higman.
Levet is especially interesting, for the type which
came into Caxton's hands about 1490, and was used
afterwards by Wynkyn de Worde in some of his
earlier books, was either obtained from him or from
the type-cutter who cut his type, for the two founts
seem to be identical. Guy Marchant is celebrated
as the printer of some curious editions of the *Dance
of Death*.

After 1490 the number of printers and stationers
increased rapidly. Panzer enumerates no fewer than

eighty-five printers, and nearly 800 books executed during the fifteenth century; and there is no doubt that his estimate is considerably under the mark. The most important productions of the Parisian press at that time were service-books, of which enormous numbers were issued. The best known publisher of such works was Simon Vostre, who, with the assistance of the printer Philip Pigouchet, began to issue *Books of Hours*, printed on vellum, with exquisite borders and illustrations. These books began to be issued about 1488, and commence with an almanac for the years 1488 to 1508. In many cases the printers did not take the trouble to make new almanacs, but were content to copy the old; indeed, we find the same almanac in use ten years later. This has led to a great deal of confusion in the bibliography of the subject, for it is a common custom of librarians and cataloguers to ascribe the printing of a book of this class to the date which occurs first in the almanac, when there is no date given in the colophon. The most celebrated publishers of these books were Simon Vostre, Philippe Pigouchet, Antoine Verard, Thielman Kerver, Gilles Hardouyn, Guillaume Eustace, Guillaume Godard, and François Regnault. Vostre and Verard do not seem themselves to have printed, but were merely publishers, far the most important printer being Pigouchet. Of the nine or ten *Books of Hours* for the use of Sarum, printed abroad during the fifteenth century, Pigouchet probably printed half, and all but two were printed in Paris. In examining early foreign-printed English service-books, it is curious to notice that while nearly all the *Horæ* were printed at Paris, the majority of Breviaries were printed at Venice, and only two at Paris. No *Horæ* is known to have been printed at Venice.

The end of the century saw the commencement of the celebrated Ascensian press, the rival in some ways of the Aldine. The founder, Jodocus Badius Ascensius (Josse Bade of Asch), was a man of great learning, and was for a time professor of humanity at Lyons, and press-corrector to Trechsel, whose daughter he married. Trechsel died in 1498, and in 1499, at the invitation of Robert Gaguin, Badius came to Paris and established himself there as a teacher of Greek and a printer. It was not, however, till 1504 that the Ascensian press became important.

It is curious to notice that, in spite of the classical tastes of the first promoters of printing in Paris, and the enormous development of printing in that city towards the end of the fifteenth century, no Greek book was produced till 1507. Through the exertions of François Tissard of Amboise, who had studied Greek in Italy, and was anxious to introduce Greek learning into France, Gilles Gourmont set up a press provided with Greek types, and issued in 1507 a book entitled βίβλος ἡ γνωμαγυρική, a small grammatical treatise, the first Greek book printed in France. From the same press, in the year following, came the first Hebrew book printed in France, a Hebrew grammar, written by Tissard. Greek printing, however, did not flourish; the supply of type was meagre and the demand for books small,[1] and it was not till 1528, in which year *Sophocles, Aristophanes, Lucian,* and *Demosthenes* were issued, that any signs of a revival were to be seen.

Lyons was the second city in France to receive the art of printing, and it was introduced into that town by Guillaume le Roy of Liège soon after 1470. The first dated book, the *Compendium* of Innocent III., appeared in September 1473. From its colophon we learn that it was printed at the expense of Bartholomieu Buyer, a citizen of Lyons; and we know from other colophons that the press was set up in Buyer's house. Bernard doubts whether Buyer was himself a printer, though he is certainly mentioned as such in several books, such as *La légende dorée* of 1476, *Le miroir de vie humaine,* and *La légende des saintz* of 1477, which are described in their colophons as 'imprimés par Bartholomieu Buyer.' His name is not found in any book after 1483, so that it is usually supposed that he died about that date. Le Roy continued to print alone for some years, but had ceased before 1493, in which year we know that he was still alive.

After Lyons comes Toulouse; and the first dated book issued there was the *Repetitio solemnis rubrice*

---

[1] Aleander in 1512, in the preface to his *Lexicon Græco-Latinum,* complained that the stock of Greek type was so meagre, that sometimes letters had to be left out here and there, and the work was often at a standstill for days.

de fide instrumentorum, 20th June 1476. It was not till 1479 that a printer's name appears in the colophon to a work by Johannes Alphonsus de Benevento. The printer, Jean Parix, was a native of Heidelberg. He had founts both of Gothic and Roman type, the Gothic being especially remarkable for the shapes of the letters, which are very distinctive, and though eccentric in form they are not at all unpleasing in appearance. In 1488, Henry Mayer began to print, issuing in that year a translation of the *De consolatione philosophiæ* of Boethius, 'en romance,' and the first French translation of the *Imitatio Christi*. This Henry Mayer has often been quoted as the first printer at Tolosa in Spain, owing to the name Tolosa in the colophons being considered to stand for that town, and not, as it really does, for Toulouse. M. Claudin, however, has found in the town registers of Toulouse a mention of Henry Mayer as a printer in 1488; and in the imprint of the *Boethius* which he printed in the same year it is distinctly stated that it was 'impresso en Tolosa de Francia.' At the end of the *Cronica de España*, printed by Mayer in 1489, is a long peroration addressed to Queen Isabella as his sovereign by Mayer, from which it is sometimes argued that the book was printed in Spain. The real fact is that the book is an exact reprint, peroration and all, of the edition printed at Seville in 1482 by Dachaver, with the sole difference that Mayer has substituted his name for that of the Spanish printer.

Angers [Feb. 5, 1476-77], Chablis [April 1, 1478],

Vienne [1478], and Poitiers [1479], are the four remaining towns into which printing was introduced before 1480. The first book issued at Angers, printed by Johannes de Turre and Morelli, is an edition of Cicero's *Rhetorica Nova*, printed in a curious Roman type, apparently copied from that used by Kaiser and Stoll at Paris. The first printer at Chablis was Pierre le Rouge; but some time after 1483 he removed to Paris, and his place was taken by Guillaume le Rouge, who moved about 1492 to Troyes, and finally also settled in Paris. Johannes Solidi and Peter Schenck are the two most important of the early printers at Vienne. Solidi was the first; but Schenck, who began in 1481, printed the most interesting books, and always in French. Two of these are of great rarity, *L'Abuze en court* and *Le hystoire de Griseldis*. The first book printed at Poitiers, the *Breviarium Historiale*, 1479, has no printer's name, nor indeed have any of the earlier books. Hain [*13,811] gives a book, *Casus longi super sextum decretalium*, printed by John and Stephen de Gradibus in 1483. The discovery of some fragments of *Heures à l'usage de l'eglise d'Angers*, with the names of the printers, Jean Bouyer et Pierre Bellescullée, printed partly in the types of the first books, make it possible that these two may have been the printers. The fragments were found in the binding of a book by M. Delisle.

Caen was the first town in Normandy where printing was practised, but only one book was printed there in the fifteenth century. It is an edition of

Horace, the first to appear in France, and of the very greatest rarity, only three copies being known, one of which, printed on vellum, is in the Spencer Library. The printers were Jacobus Durandas and Egidius Quijoue, and the book was issued 6th June 1480. It is a quarto of forty leaves, with twenty lines to the page, printed in a good, bold Gothic type. There were several privileged booksellers attached to the University of Caen, but it is improbable that any of them printed, at any rate in the fifteenth century. They obtained their books from either Paris or Rouen.

Within the next seven years ten towns set up presses in the following order:—Albi (1481), Chartres (1482), Metz (1482), Troyes (1483), Chambéry (1484), Bréhant - Loudéac (1484), Rennes (1484), Tréguier (1485), Salins (1485), Abbeville (1486).

At Albi, on 17th November 1481, the wonderful edition of the *Meditationes* of Turrecremata, supposed to have been printed by Numeister, was issued. This was preceded by a book of *Æneas Sylvius*, without date, but ascribed to the same printer, though printed with a different type; and Hain [8723] quotes a third book, also without date, *Historia septem sapientum*. The arguments of M. Claudin, who has written a book to prove that Numeister was the printer at Albi, though ingenious, are very far from conclusive.

Two books were executed at Chartres in the fifteenth century, a *Missal* in 1482 and a *Breviary* in 1483, both for the use of that diocese. The printer was Jean du Pré of Paris.

The first printers at Metz, Johannes Colini and Gerhardus de Novacivitate, who printed in 1482 an edition of the *Imitatio Christi*, used a very peculiar type of Gothic with a number of Roman capitals mixed with it, resembling that of Nicholas Götz at Cologne, and which, leaving Cologne in 1480, appeared at Treves in 1481. In 1499, Caspar Hochfeder came to Metz from Nuremberg.

The earliest book with the name of Troyes in the colophon is a *Breviarium secundum usum ecclesiæ Trecensis*, of 25th September 1483. It was executed by Pierre le Rouge, who probably came over from Chablis for the purpose. In 1492, Guillaume le Rouge, who had before this printed at Chablis, set up the first permanent press in the town.

Bréhant-Loudéac was the first town in Brittany where books were printed; and from 1484 to 1485 the two printers, Robin Foucquet and Jean Crès, issued ten books, all in French, in a ragged Gothic type. The first printers at Abbeville, Jean du Pré of Paris and Pierre Gérard, to judge by their books, were well-skilled workmen, for both the printing and illustrations are very fine. Their first book was an edition of the *Somme Rurale*, and it was followed by a splendid edition, in two volumes, of *La cité de Dieu* of Augustine, a large folio with wonderful woodcuts. Their third work was *Le Triomphe des neuf Preux;* and this is the last book known to have been printed at Abbeville in the fifteenth century.

Though Rouen was without a printer till 1487, it

became within a very few years one of the most important towns in the history of French printing. Its
fortunate position on the Seine, equally advantageous
for sending books to Paris or exporting them to
England, was doubtless the chief cause of its great
prosperity, and its influence over the book trade was
felt, not only over all France, but over England as
well.   The first printer was Guillaume le Talleur, and
his first book, *Les Chroniques de Normandie*, was published in May 1487.   He printed several law books for
Richard Pynson about 1490, and was very probably
his teacher.   The most important export from Rouen
was certainly service-books, and of these endless
numbers were issued for various uses.   Martin Morin,
who began to print in 1490, was especially connected
with this kind of work, and some of the most beautiful of the Salisbury Missals are from his press.   The
printers were, however, not nearly so numerous as
the booksellers, though it is not always very easy to
distinguish between them.   Morin, Le Talleur, Noel
de Harsy, Jean le Bourgeois, and Jacques le Forestier, may safely be given as printers ; others, like
Richard and Regnault, were probably only booksellers or stationers.   Besançon also had a printing
press in 1487, but who the first printer was is not
very certainly known.   Several writers consider him to
have been Jean du Pré ; but M. Thierry-Poux, judging from the types, considers that Peter Metlinger,
who printed later at Dôle, is more likely to have been
the printer.   In 1488 (26th March 1487), Jean Crès

printed the first book at Lantenac, an edition in French of *Mandeville's Travels.* Its colophon mentions no name of place, but the type and the printer's name are identical with those of the *Doctrinal des nouvelles mariées* of 1491, which has the name of the place, Lantenac, in the colophon.

Between 1490 and the end of 1500 printing was introduced into twenty towns. In 1490, to Embrun, Grenoble, and Dôle ; but the first and second of these places only produced a single book each. In 1491, to Orleans, Goupillières, Angoulême, Dijon, and Narbonne.

M. Jarry[1] mentions a certain Jehan le Roy, who was spoken of at Orleans in 1481 as a printer and stationer, but nothing printed by him is known. The first book known is a *Manipulus Curatorum* in French, printed by Matthew Vivian. Our knowledge of the existence of a press at Goupillières in the fifteenth century is the result of a fortunate discovery made by M. Delisle. He found, used as boards for an old binding, thirty-six leaves of a book of *Hours 'à l'usage du diocèse d'Évreux,'* with a colophon stating that it was printed at Goupillières on the 8th May 1491, by Michel Andrieu, a priest. At Narbonne also but one book was printed before 1500, a *Breviarium ad usum ecclesiæ Narbonensis.*

In 1492, printing was introduced into Cluni ; and in 1493, to Nantes, Châlons, Tours, and Mâcon. Châlons and Mâcon are each represented by one

---

[1] *Les débuts de l'Imprimerie à Orléans.* Orléans, 1884.

book, which in each case is a *Diurnale* for the use of
its own church.

In 1495, Jean Berton began to print at Limoges,
issuing service-books for the use of the church. The
last six towns to be mentioned are Provins (1496),
Valence (1496), Avignon (1497), Périgueux (1498),
Perpignan (1500), and Valenciennes (1500).

Nothing seems to have resulted from the early
attempts at printing at Avignon, which have been
spoken of before, and the first dated book issued
there is an edition of part of *Lucian*, printed for
Nicholas Tepe, by Jean du Pré of Lyons, on the 15th
October 1497.

It will be noticed that printing was introduced into
many of the provincial towns of France merely to
serve a temporary purpose, and not for the object
of permanent work. In many cases the printer was
brought to the town, probably at the request and
expense of the ecclesiastical authorities, to print such
service-books as were required for the use of the
church.   For this reason we find printers and types
moving from place to place, so that it is not always
easy to assign a book to a particular town, when the
type in which it is printed was used in several places.
The splendid series of facsimiles edited by M. Thierry-
Poux, and published by order of the Government,
gives great assistance to the study of French typography ; while from time to time small monographs
have appeared giving the history of printing in all the
more important towns of France.

CHAPTER VI.

THE LOW COUNTRIES.

On no subject connected with printing has more been written, and to less purpose, than on the Haarlem invention of printing by Lourens Janszoon Coster. During the fifteenth century much had been said about the invention, accrediting it always to Germany; and it was not till 1499 that a reference was made to an earlier Dutch discovery in the following passage of the *Cologne Chronicle* : [1]—

'This highly valuable art was discovered first of all in Germany, at Mentz on the Rhine. And it is a great honour to the German nation that such ingenious men are found among them. And it took place about the year of our Lord 1440 ; and from this time until the year 1450, the art and what is connected with it was being investigated. And in the year of our Lord 1450 it was a golden year [jubilee], and they began to print, and the first book they printed was the Bible in Latin ; it was printed in a large letter, resembling the letter with which at present missals are printed. Although the art [as has been said] was discovered at Mentz, in the manner as it is now generally used, yet the first prefiguration was found in Holland [the Netherlands], in the *Donatuses*, which were printed there before that time. And from these *Donatuses* the beginning of the said art was taken, and it was invented in a manner much more masterly and subtile than this,

---

[1] *The Haarlem Legend*, by Dr. Van der Linde, translated by J. H. Hessels. London, 1871, 8vo, p. 8.

and became more and more ingenious. One named Omnibonus wrote in a preface to the book called *Quinctilianus*, and in some other books too, that a Walloon from France, named Nicol. Jenson, discovered first of all this masterly art; but that is untrue, for there are those still alive who testify that books were printed at Venice before Nicol. Jenson came there and began to cut and make letters. But the first inventor of printing was a citizen of Mentz, born at Strasburg, and named Junker Johan Gutenberg. From Mentz the art was introduced first of all into Cologne, then into Strasburg, and afterwards into Venice. The origin and progress of the art was told me verbally by the honourable Master Ulrich Zell of Hanau, still printer at Cologne, anno 1499, and by whom the said art came to Cologne.'

This narrative, it will be seen, breaks down, if we examine its accuracy strictly, in several places. To get over this apparent difficulty, we are told that the compiler of the Chronicle took the various parts of his statement from various sources. The statement that printing was invented at Mainz, from Hartmann Schedel's *Nuremberg Chronicle* of 1493; that from 1440 to 1450 it was being investigated, is an addition of his own; that about 1450 people began to print, and that the first book printed was the *Bible* in Latin, was told him by Ulric Zel, and so on. But evidence which on certain points is inaccurate, cannot be implicitly trusted on other points; and since it is impossible to trust absolutely the statement of the Chronicle, we must seek information from the best source, that is, the earliest productions of the press.

Coster himself was not heard of as a printer till about a hundred years after he was supposed to have printed, when Junius wrote in his *Batavia* the wonderful legend of the letters cut in beech bark.

That a person called Lourens Janszoon lived at Haarlem from 1436 to 1483 seems to be an established fact ; but, at the same time, all the entries and notices relating to him show that he was a chandler or innkeeper. Von der Linde very justly, therefore, considers he was not a printer ; and this view is certainly reasonable, for we can hardly suppose that a man could have printed all the so-called Costeriana and at the same time have attended to his business so carefully, that all the entries which relate to him speak of him only as an innkeeper, and no mention of any kind is made of him as a printer, though he was, so believers in him assert, the only printer in Holland for thirty years.

Coming to the books themselves, what do we find ? The first printed date is 1473, in which year books were issued at both Utrecht and Alost. M. Holtrop mentions that the Hague copy of the *Tractatus Gulielmi de Saliceto de salute corporis et animæ* and *Yliada* was bought by a certain Abbat Conrad for the library of his house ; and as the Abbat in question was Abbat only from 1471 to 1474, the book cannot have been printed later than 1471–74 ; and this and the rubricated 1472 in the Darmstadt copy of the *Saliceto* are at present the only dates which we can use for our purposes.

There are, however, a large number of fragments of books known, printed in a rude type and with the appearance of early printing, all of which are frequently asserted to have been printed before 1473.

G

These books, consisting for the most part of editions
of the *Donatus* or the *Doctrinale*, are known by the
name of Costeriana, as being the supposed productions of Coster. Among them also are the four
editions of the *Speculum*, which we have examined
at length in Chapter I. Fragments of at least fifty
books or editions are known, which may be separated
by their types into eight groups. Concerning the
types Mr. Hessels says: 'Type 2 is inseparably connected with type 1; and as the former is so much
like type 3 that some consider these two types
identical, nothing would be gained by separating
them. Type 4 and 5 occur in one and the same
book; and as certain letters of type 5 are identical
with some of type 3, they may all be linked together.
Type 6 is identical with type 5 except the P, which
is larger and of a different form. Types 7 and 8 are
linked on to the types 1–6, on account of the great
family-likeness between them, they all having that
peculiar perpendicular stroke to the cross-bar of the *t*,
and a down stroke or curl attached to the *r*, which
is found in no other types of the Netherlands.'

The close connection of all these types points to
the books having been produced in one place; but
where this one place was, cannot be determined.
The account written by Junius, in 1568, of the invention of printing by Coster, mentions Haarlem as
the place where he printed, and they have therefore
been always ascribed to Haarlem by such writers as
believe in the Costerian invention. Mr. Bradshaw,

Inf̃ertur nũquã trãſfiq cõſtructio plena
Filius alphei iacobiq maria quuestãtt
Cõſtrue ſic caſũ ſi ſit ꝓone vocãtẽ
Nox reatũ ponis hĩne pſonale locabis
Perbũ quod fĩns ſtatues ſi ꝛetera deſint
Terñus hĩne caſus ⁊ ꝗtus ſepe ſequũt
Quẽ vbo ſubdes adũbia ſubde ſecundũ
Caſum rectori debet vor ꝗoſitiua
Ei varto ꝓiungi vel ſerto que regit iꝑſa
Infinitiuũ ꝓſois ſiue quibuſdam
Des adiectiuis vt ſũt abiles piger egꝛ
Hãc olim pulcrã veteres direre figurã
Perba ſi ſunt debꝝ ſubꝝ audet woltꝝ poteſtꝝ
Nitiſ ⁊ temptaſt dignat ſitꝝ mouetꝝ
Inꝓiſt ⁊ tedet piget ⁊ pudet atꝝ meret
Et ꝑer aſt gaudet delectat penitet vrget
Et ꝑaꝗ ⁊ diſtit de cett ⁊ ſilet ⁊ licet adde
Que ꝓdicta notãt ⁊ que cõtraria ſignãt
Addere mlta potes ꝗꝛto caſu ꝑeunte
Que iũgres vbo iũgres et ꝓinpianti
Si genest verbi ſua ſignificatio ſias
Conſona debetur iꝑſi cõſtructio vꝑrbi
Sed pſonale ſuꝑponẽs rectus habebis
Quẽ ablatiui ꝑeunt rectore ſoluti
Quẽ poſtponũtur ſed vir interſectis illos
Appellans chuun ſubſtãtiuũꝝ hoꝝ
Dum retineſ poſt ſe rectꝗ gñiꝝ locabiſ
Et ſubſtãtiui dura ſignificãno veꝑiſ
Aſſiuis ⁊ ſepe ſoleſ cõſtructiot ꝑdr
Quẽ ꝗlis quãtus aut cuias ꝗtis ⁊ ꝗt
Si illa relatiue penitus ꝓponeꝛ deben̄
Obliqis verbo ꝓiũgres miſſa rogant

who refused to assign books to particular places without reason, said : ' I am compelled to leave the *Speculum* at Utrecht until I know anything positive to the contrary, because it is at Utrecht that the cuts first appear, cut up into pieces in a book printed by Veldener at that place in 1481.' This statement does not mean that the Costeriana were necessarily printed at Utrecht, but that the place where we find the materials as soon as they can be connected with any place, is Utrecht, and that therefore such little evidence as exists is in favour of these books having been printed there. One point which tells in favour of Utrecht, is the fact that one of the Costeriana is a *Donatus* in French, and Utrecht is one of the few places in the Netherlands where such a book is likely to have been produced.

There is no direct evidence in favour of Haarlem or Utrecht ; and indirect evidence is not particularly in favour of Haarlem, unless it is considered that some belief may be placed in Junius' wonderful narrative. It is certainly wiser to leave the matter open, or, with Bradshaw, place the books provisionally at Utrecht till we have a better reason for placing them elsewhere.

The more important question as to the date when these Costeriana were produced, seems still as far as ever from any satisfactory solution. Mr. Hessels takes them back to 1446 by the ingenious method of putting eighteen months between each edition. This method of working is based on no sound principle, and leads to no result of any value. Another argument of Mr. Hessels, and one that is hardly worthy of so learned a writer, is that since the Costeriana look older than the first Mainz books, therefore they are older. The foolishness of this reasoning is too apparent to need any explanation, for it amounts to the assertion that the same phase of development in different countries means the same date. But if the earliest dated books of the Low Countries are compared with the productions of Germany, it needs a prejudiced eye to see in the former any approach to the exquisite beauty and regularity of the German type and printing.

There is one point which seems to me to argue strongly against the early date ascribed to the Costeriana. They were produced by ordinary typographic processes, such as would be used for printing any book, and there is little or no improvement observable in the latest compared with the earliest. Yet, during the thirty years to which these books are ascribed, no work of any size or importance was produced from this press. It can hardly be assumed that during these years there was no demand for books, when we consider that immediately after 1473 books of all kinds were produced in great number. Nor can we reasonably suppose that the great demand for the *Donatus* and the *Doctrinale* ceased about 1473. The printing of school-books did not require to be ornamental, for they had to be produced as cheaply as possible, so that this class of work naturally soon fell into the hands of the poorer printers. We see many examples of this in studying the history of printing in other places, and find the finest and the rudest work being produced side by side. Block-books and xylographic *Donatuses* were printed in Germany up to the last years of the fifteenth century, as old in appearance as the productions of fifty years earlier. We may connect certain of these Costeriana with the years 1471–74, within which period printing presses were started at Utrecht and Alost; but why should all the rest be placed earlier? It is curious that, while we have no dates forcing us to fix them early, neither have we dates preventing us from fixing them late.

Because certain of these books were written by Pius II., who became Pope in 1458, Mr. Hessels seizes on 1458 as one of the dates we may take as relating to their printing, and groups the Costeriana round that date. He might equally well have grouped others round the fourth century, when Ælius Donatus lived, or round 1207, when Alexander de Villa Dei finished his *Doctrinale*. The only date as regards the printing of a book that can be derived from the authorship is a date before which the book cannot have been printed. M. Dziatzko mentions one point which he considers conclusive as giving a late date to the Costeriana. In them is *wrongly* used a particular form of the letter x, which is not found in Dutch manuscripts, and which was used at the first Mainz press for a special purpose.

Putting aside, then, the useless mass of conjecture and sophistry that obscures the subject, the case stands thus. The first printed date in the Low Countries is 1473, and there are a group of undated books which may perhaps be placed before or round this date; beyond this we have no information whatever.

Before leaving this subject, it is worth noticing that there is a simple explanation for the fact that almost all the Costeriana fragments are on vellum. They have in most cases been found in the bindings of books, and it was the almost invariable habit of Netherlandish binders to line the boards of their bindings with vellum. They used if possible clean vellum, or printed or written only on one side, the used side being pasted down and the clean side exposed. In this way many indulgences have been preserved.

In 1473, printing starts simultaneously at Utrecht and Alost, and from that time onward its history is clear. More attention has been paid to the history of printing in the Netherlands than to that of any other country, and the work of Holtrop, Campbell, and Bradshaw offers a firm foundation to rest upon.

The first printers at Utrecht were Nicholas Ketelaer and Gerard de Leempt, and their first book was the *Historia Scholastica* of Petrus Comestor. Though they printed a large number of books, only three are dated, two in 1473 and one in 1474. About 1475 a printer named William Hees printed some books at

Utrecht; and in 1478, Veldener moved to that town from Louvain, where he had been printing up to that time.

The first printer at Alost was Thierry Martens, an accomplished linguist and scholar, who is supposed by many bibliographers to have learned to print at Venice. He says in the colophon to the *De vita beata libellus* of Baptista Mantuanus—

> 'Hoc opus impressi Martins Theodoricus Alosti,
> Qui Venetum scita Flandrensibus affero cuncta.'

On this basis the story has arisen, and it is perhaps hardly sufficient to justify the conclusions. The first books, four in number, printed in 1473 and the beginning of 1474, were printed in partnership with John of Westphalia, a printer who in 1474 migrated to Louvain. Thierry Martens continued by himself at Alost for a while, but moved on, in 1493, to Antwerp, and in 1498 to Louvain. According to Van der Meersch, he left Louvain in 1502 to return to Antwerp, but left this town again in 1512, and settled definitely at Louvain till the end of his career in 1529.

Printing was introduced at Louvain in 1474, and it is, after Antwerp, the most important town in that respect in the Low Countries. The first printer was John of Westphalia,[1] whom we have just mentioned as a printer at Alost in partnership with Thierry

---

[1] John de Paderborn de Westphalia was in 1473 still a scribe, for in that year he wrote a MS. of the *Scala* of Johannes Climacus at and for the Augustinian House at Marpach.

Martens. He seems to have been the owner of the type used at Alost, for he continued to print with it, and in June 1474 issued the *Commentariolus de pleuresi* by Antonius Guainerius, the first book known to have been issued at Louvain. John of Westphalia continued to print up to the year 1496; and Campbell[1] enumerates over one hundred and eighty books as having been printed by him in these twenty-two years. In some of his books we find a small woodcut portrait of himself, used first in the *Justinian* of 1475; and a few of his books have the red initial letters printed in by hand. John Veldener, the second printer at Louvain, was matriculated at the university there, in the faculty of medicine, 30th July 1473. His first book was probably the *Consolatio peccatorum* of Jacobus de Theramo, which contains a prefatory letter, addressed 'Johanni Veldener artis impressoriæ magistro,' dated 7th Aug. 1474. Veldener continued to print at Louvain till 1478, and he is found in that year at Utrecht, where he printed till 1481. After this he moved to Kuilenburg, issuing books there in 1483 and 1484.

Besides those that have been mentioned, seven other printers worked at Louvain before the close of the fifteenth century. These were—Conrad Braem (1475), Conrad de Westphalia (1476), Hermann de Nassou (1483), Rodolphe Loeffs (1483), Egidius vander Heerstraten (1484), Ludovicus de Ravescot (1487), and Thierry Martens (1498).

[1] *Annales de la Typographie Néerlandaise au xv. Siècle.* 1874. 8vo.

Bruges, one of the most prosperous and artistic of the towns in the Netherlands, is intimately associated with the history of English printing ; for it was there that our first printer, Caxton, began to print. It was not, however, a productive town as regards printing, for only two printers, or at most three, were at work there in the fifteenth century. Of these the most important was Colard Mansion. He was by profession a writer and illuminator of manuscripts, and his name is found year by year from 1454 to 1473 in the book of the Guild of St. John. It was probably about 1475 that he began to print ; but his first dated book appeared in the following year. About the years 1475–77, Caxton was in partnership with Mansion, whether generally or only for the production of certain books, we do not know. But together they printed three books, *The Recuyell of the Histories of Troye*, *The Game and playe of the Chesse*, and *Les quatre derrennieres choses*. After Caxton's departure, in 1477, Mansion continued to print by himself. It is worth noticing that in 1477 he first made use of a device. The first dated book issued by Mansion, *De la ruyne des nobles hommes et femmes*, by Boccaccio, has a curious history. It was issued first without any woodcuts, and no spaces were left for them. Then the first leaf containing the prologue was cancelled, and reprinted so as to leave a space for a cut of the author presenting his book. At a later date, the first leaves of all the books, excepting books i. and vi., were cancelled, and reissued with spaces for engravings. Mansion printed altogether about twenty-four books, the last being a moralised version of Ovid's *Metamorphoses*, issued in May 1484. Almost immediately after this book was finished, the printer fled from Bruges, and his rooms over the porch of the Church of St. Donatus were let to a book-binder named Jean Gossin. This latter paid the rent still owing by Mansion, and is supposed to have come into possession of the stock of the *Ovid*, for several copies of the book are known in which the leaves 113–218, 296–389 have been reprinted, presumably by Gossin, and these examples do not contain Mansion's device.

The other printer, Jean Brito, is little more than a name. Campbell gives four books as having been printed by him, but only one contains his name. This, however, is a book of exceptional interest, the *Instruction et doctrine de tous chrétiens et chrétiennes*, by Gerson; and but one copy is known, now in the Bibliothèque Nationale. It has the following curious colophon in verse:—

> 'Aspice presentis scripture gracia que sit
> Confer opus opere, spectetur codice codex.
> Respice quam munde, quam terse quamque decore
> Imprimit hec civis brugensis brito Johannes,
> Inveniens artem nullo monstrante mirandam
> Instrumenta quoque non minus laude stupenda.'

The last two lines, which, translated literally, say, ' Discovering, without being shown by any one, the wonderful art, and also the tools, not less objects for wonder and praise,' would seem to imply that Brito claimed to be a self-taught printer. That this may have been the case is quite possible, and it is the only reasonable interpretation to put upon the lines. They suggest, however, still a further inference. The type in which this book is printed seems to be identical with that used afterwards by William de Machlinia at Holborn, in London, and extraordinarily similar to the type used by Veldener at Utrecht. If Brito was a self-taught printer, who invented his own tools, he must also have been a type-founder; and if so, may very likely have supplied William de Machlinia with his type.

After Bruges comes Brussels, where but one press was established before 1500. This was set up by the Brothers of the Common Life, who must have found their old industry of copying manuscripts seriously interfered with by the competition of the new art. They therefore started a press at their house, called 'Nazareth,' and in 1476 issued their first dated book, the *Gnotosolitos sive speculum conscientiæ*, by Arnoldus de Gheilhoven, a large folio of 472 leaves. From 1476 to 1484[1] they worked industriously, producing about thirty-five books, only one of which clearly states who and what the printers were. This is the *Legenda Henrici Imperatoris et Kunigundis Imperatricis* of 1484, where we read in the colophon: . . . 'impresse in famosa civitate bruxellensi per fratres communis

---

[1] A book of 1487 is quoted by Lambinet, but the date has probably been either misprinted or misread.

vite in nazareth' . . . There is no doubt that, as types come to be studied and recognised, more books will be found printed by this Brotherhood. Other establishments of the same Order had practised, or were shortly to practise, the art of printing. That at Marienthal, important in the history of printing, had been at work for some years; others at Rostock, Nuremberg, and Gouda were to follow; while, as we have seen, if we are to believe M. Madden, the monastery at Weidenbach was the instructor of all the more noted printers of Europe. The similarity in appearance between the Brussels type and that of Ther Hoernen at Cologne is very striking, and has deceived even M. Van der Meersch, Ther Hoernen's bibliographer. The distinguishing mark of this type, or the one most readily to be distinguished, is a very voluminous capital S in the later books.

Gerard Leeu, the first printer at Gouda, is the most important of all the Low Country printers of the fifteenth century. His first book was issued in 1477, a Dutch edition of the *Epistles and Gospels;* and five other books followed in the same year. His first illustrated book, the *Dialogus creaturarum moralisatus*, was issued in 1480. About the middle of the year 1484 he removed to Antwerp, and printed there till 1493. In that year, while the *Chronicles of England* were being printed, a letter-cutter named Henric van Symmen, one of Leeu's workmen, struck work. In a quarrel which followed, Leeu was struck on the head, and died after three days' illness. The workman who gave the blow was fined forty gulden, not a very heavy punishment for manslaughter. At the end of the *Chronicles* the workmen put the following colophon: 'Enprentyd . . . by maister Gerard de Leew, a man of grete wysedom in all mancr of kunnying: whych nowe is come from lyfe unto the deth, which is grete harme for many a poure man. On whos sowle god almyghty for hys hygh grace have mercy. Amen.'

Leeu must have employed a good deal of labour, for he printed a very large number of books; Campbell gives about two hundred, and his numbers are always being added to. But what makes Leeu especially interesting to us is the fact of his printing English books. Of these, he issued seven between 1486 and 1493—a Grammar, two Sarum Service-books, and four other popular books which will be noticed later.

Another interesting printer who was settled at Gouda was Gotfried de Os, whom Bradshaw considers to have been identical with Govaert van Ghemen. He began to print at Gouda in 1486, but about 1490 removed to Copenhagen, printing at Leyden on his way. Before he went there he parted with some of his printing materials, type, initial letters, and woodcuts, which came into the hands of W. de Worde, and were used in England.

Five other towns in the Netherlands possessed printing presses before 1480—Deventer (1477), Delft

(1477), St. Maartensdyk (1478), Nymegen (1479), and Zwolle (1479).

At Deventer there were only two printers, R. Paffroed and J. de Breda; but between them they printed at least five hundred books, about a quarter of the whole number issued in the Netherlands in the fifteenth century.

At St. Maartensdyk in Zeeland only one book was printed, *Der zyelen troeste*, the work of a printer named Peter Werrecoren, in November 1478. Of this book only one copy is known, preserved in the library of the abbey of Averbode. In the colophon the printer apologises for the short-comings of his book, saying that it is his first, and that he hopes by the grace of God to improve. We have, however, no record of his ever printing again. Nymegen had also but one printer, Gerard Leempt, who issued four books. Zwolle, where Peter van Os of Breda printed from 1479 onwards, is an interesting place in the history of printing, for there, in 1487, appeared portions of the original blocks of the *Biblia Pauperum* used to illustrate a Dutch edition of the *Epistles and Gospels*, and in 1494 a block from the *Canticum Canticorum*. Peregrinus Barmentlo, the only printer at Hasselt, was at work from 1480 to 1490. He seems to have had some connection with Peter van Os, as was only natural from the situation of Hasselt and its nearness to Zwolle; and we find the cuts of one printer in the hands of the other.

Arend de Keysere commenced to print at Auden-

arde in 1480, his first book being the *Sermons* of
Hermannus de Petra. By April 1483 he had moved
from Audenarde and settled at Ghent, where he
remained till his death in 1489. His wife, Beatrice
van Orrior, continued to print for a short time, but
no copy is known of any of her productions. At a
later date she married again, her husband being a
certain Henry van den Dale, who is mentioned in
the St. Lucas-gilde book at Bruges as a printer in
that town in 1505–6.

In the fifteenth century more printers were settled
in Antwerp than in any other Netherlandish town.
The first to settle there was Matthew van der
Goes, and his first book is dated 29th April 1482.
In the same year he issued the *Bœck van Tondalus
vysioen*, which has the misprinted date 1472, and
has for that reason been sometimes quoted as the
first book printed in the Low Countries, or more
often as the first book printed with signatures.
We have already spoken of Gerard Leeu, who was
the next to settle at Antwerp; and shortly after
his appearance in 1484, Nicolas Kesler of Basle
opened a shop there for the sale of his books. There
are said to be three books with Kesler's name, and
the name of Antwerp given as the town; and though
his press at Basle was at work without a break from
1486 onward, still in 1488 his name appears amongst
the list of members of the St. Lucas-gilde at Antwerp.
It is very probable, as Campbell suggests, that Kesler
was entered as a member to enable him to sell

his books in Antwerp. The most interesting among
the remaining printers of the town was Thierry
Martens, who began to print in 1493, and stayed till
1497. His various movements have been spoken of
before. Leyden, Ghent, Kuilenburg, and Haarlem
all started presses in 1483. The first printer of
Haarlem, Bellaert, seems to have obtained his
materials for the most part from Leeu, both type and
woodcuts ; but the town cannot have been a flourish-
ing one from a printer's point of view; for, though
another workman, Joh: Andreæ, printed a few books
in 1486, both presses disappear after that year.
At Bois-le-duc, Gerard Leempt, from Nÿmegen,
printed a few books between 1484 and 1490. In
1495 the Canons of St. Michael's in den Hem, near
Shoenhoven, began to print books in order to obtain
means to rebuild their convent, which had been
destroyed by fire the year before. They printed one
or two editions of the *Breviary* of different uses, but
the rest of their books were all in the vernacular.
Schiedam was the last town in the Netherlands
where printing was practised before 1500, and there,
about 1498, an unknown printer issued a very remarkable book.

There were altogether in the Netherlands twenty-
two towns whence books were issued before 1500,
and in this list it will be noticed that Haarlem stands
near the end. When printing had once been introduced it spread rapidly, all but three towns starting
within the first ten years.

CHAPTER VII.

THE first book printed in Spain, according to some authorities, is a small volume of poems by Bernardo Fenollar and others, written in honour of the Virgin on the occasion of a congress held at Valentia in March 1474. It is said to have been printed in that town in the same year; but it has never been fully described, nor is it known where a copy is preserved.

According to M. Salvá, the first two books printed in Spain with a certain date are the *Comprehensorium* (23rd February 1475), and the *Sallust* (13th July 1475), both printed at Valentia. As, however, the year began on Easter Day, the second book is really the earlier, and with it the authentic history of printing in Spain begins. The book itself is a small quarto, printed in Roman letter, without signatures or catchwords, and but two copies seem to be known, one in the Royal Library of Madrid, the other in the Barberini Library at Rome. The printers were Lambert Palmart, a German, and Alonzo Fernandez of Cordova; but their names are found, for the first time, in a *Bible* of 1478 known only from

H

four leaves, one of them fortunately containing the colophon. It is very probable that Alonzo Fernandez, whose name only occurs in this one colophon, was not a printer, though it is not known in what capacity he was associated with Palmart. He was certainly known as a celebrated astronomer. Lambert Palmart continued to print at Valentia up to the year 1494, and by that time other printers had settled in the town. Jacobus de Villa is mentioned by Panzer in 1493 and 1495; and in this latter year we find also Peter Hagembach, who later on, at Toledo, printed the celebrated *Mozarabic Missal* and *Breviary*.

In 1475 a certain Matthæus Flandrus printed an edition of the *Manipulus Curatorum* at Saragossa. He is supposed to have been a wandering printer, and considered by some to be the Matthew Vendrell who printed at Barcelona in 1482, and at Gerona in 1483. Between 1475 and 1485 no book is known to have been printed at Saragossa; but in the latter year a press was started by Paul Hurus, a native of Constance, who printed till almost the end of the fifteenth century, and was followed by three Germans, George Cock, Leonard Butz, and Lupus Appentegger.

Seville was the third city of Spain where printing was practised, and the first dated book issued there was the *Sacramental* of Clemente Sanchez de Vercial, printed by three partners, Anton Martinez, Bartholomé Segura, and Alphonso del Puerto, in 1477. An undated edition of the same work is ascribed by

Mendez and others to an earlier date, and a third edition was issued in May 1478. Another book, the *Manuale seu Repertorium super Abbatem Panormitanum per Alphonsum Diaz de Montalvo*, was issued by the same printers in the same year. Hain mentions sixteen printers who worked in Seville during the fifteenth century ; and of these many were Germans.

The first printers at Barcelona were Peter Brun and Nicholas Spindeler, who issued, in 1478, two books by Aquinas, commentaries on parts of Aristotle. These are almost certainly the first two books printed in that town, though a large number of supposititious books, with dates from 1473 onwards, are quoted by different writers. Amongst other printers who worked at Barcelona may be mentioned John Rosembach of Heidelberg, who paid visits to various towns, being found at Tarragona in 1499, and at Perpignan in 1500. Another printer, Jaques de Gurniel, left Barcelona about the end of the century and went to Valladolid, where he printed during the first years of the sixteenth century.

The first book printed at Lerida has a curious history. It is a *Breviary*, according to the use of the church at Lerida, printed by a German, Henry Botel, in 1479, and the whole expense of its publication was undertaken by a certain Antonio Palares, the bell-ringer of the church. It is an extremely rare book ; but there is a copy of it in the Bodleian Library, and another in the Carmelite convent at

Barcelona. Two other books were printed in this town in the fifteenth century, but they bear no printer's name ; they are both commentaries on parts of Aristotle by Petrus de Castrovol, and were printed in 1488 and 1489.

A book is quoted by Caballero as having been printed at Segorbe in 1479, the *Constitutiones synodales Bartholomæi Marti;* but its existence is a little doubtful. Besides this one book, no other is known to have been printed at Segorbe until well on in the sixteenth century ; and it is therefore quite probable that the book, if it really exists, was printed at some other town, and that the writer who saw it was misled by the occurrence of the name in the title.

Printing is said to have been introduced at Toledo in 1480. The book which bears this date, *Leyes originales de los Reyes de España*, has no name of place, but has been assigned to Toledo by several Spanish bibliographers who have examined a copy, and who are clear that it is printed in the same type as the *Confutatorium errorum* of Peter Ximenes de Prexamo, which was printed there by John Vasqui in July 1486. This latter book has been considered by many to be the first, since, as it was written by a canon of Toledo in 1478, it is argued that had that city possessed a press it would have been issued before 1486.

Salamanca, Zamora, Gerona, follow in 1481, 1482, and 1483 respectively, though the existence of a press at the last place is very doubtful. The one book said to have been printed there, *Memorial del pecador remut*, has the following words in the colophon : 'impressa a despeses de Matheu Vendrell mercader en la ciutat de Girona.' This Matthew Vendrell appears also at Barcelona in 1484; but he seems to have been a stationer rather than a printer, and the wording of the colophon mentioned above tends to confirm that idea. Unfortunately, the very great rarity of early Spanish books, at any rate in this country, precludes the comparative study of the types, and very little has yet been done to distinguish them. If this were done, it would be easy to settle the printers of such doubtful books. As there is no other book known to have been printed at Gerona till near the middle of the sixteenth century, it will be safer, until a fuller account be forthcoming, to ascribe this book, following M. Nèe de la Rochelle, to a press at Barcelona.

In 1485 we have Burgos, where Frederick of Basle (at one time an associate of Wenssler's) printed ; Palma, where Nicolas Calafati printed ; and probably also Xeres, though the existence of the press in this latter place is doubtful. The only known book quoted by M. Caballero is the *Constitutiones synodales urbis vel ecclesiæ Xericanæ*, per Barth: Marti, 1485. This bibliographer, however, gives no information about the book, or any indication of the size or type ; and as no other book is known to have been printed at Xeres within the next fifty years, it is quite probable that the book mentioned above, though relating to the town, was not printed there.

At Murcia only two or three books were issued in the fifteenth century, printed by a German named Lope de Roca. The first is the *Copilacion de las Batallas campales*, finished the 28th of May 1487. Panzer, Maittaire, and others speak erroneously of the printer as Juan de Roca. Lope de Roca, after printing two or three books in Murcia, left there and went to Valentia, where he printed in 1495 and 1497.

In 1489, printing was introduced into San Cucufat, into Coria, where only one book was printed in the fifteenth century, the *Blason general de todas las insignias del universo*, printed by Bartholomeus de Lila (Lille), a Fleming ; and it is usually said into Tolosa. The history of printing in the latter town offers many difficulties. Bibliographers have confused Toulouse in France with Tolosa in Biscay ; and the difficulty increases when we find that some Spanish books were certainly printed at the former place. The best authorities seem unfortunately to agree that the *Cronica de España*, by Diego de Valera, is the earliest book ; printed by Henry Meyer or Mayer in 1489. M. Nèe de la Rochelle speaks of this *Chronicle* as printed in 1488, and also quotes a work by Guillaume de Deguilleville, a translation into Spanish of the *Pelerinage de la vie humaine*, printed by the same printer as early as 1480. The date should be 1490, but is given as 1480 in the *Bibl. Hisp. vetus* of

Antonio (ii. 311), and also by Hain (No. 7848). This Henry Mayer, however, was certainly a printer of Toulouse in France, and not of Tolosa, so that all the remarks of the bibliographers are beside the point. His name is found mentioned in 1488 in registers at Toulouse ; and he says in the colophon to the *Boethius* of the same year, 'impresso en Tolosa de Francia.' It is not at all improbable that all the early books with 'Tolosæ' in the colophon were printed in France, and that there was no fifteenth century press at Tolosa.

The first book printed at Valladolid is the *Tractado breve de Confession* of 1492 ; but it has no printer's name. In the following year another book was printed, which gives the name of the printer as Johan de Francour. The next two places, Cagliari and Monterey, have each only one book printed in the fifteenth century. The book printed at Cagliari is a *Speculum Ecclesiæ*, and was printed by Salvador de Bolonga (Bologna), at the request of Nicholas Dagreda. The only known copy is in the Municipal Library at Palma. The book printed at Monterey was a *Missal*, printed by two partners, Gundisalvus Rodericus de la Passera and Johannes de Porres. Granada (1496), Tarragona (1498), the Monastery of the Blessed Virgin of Monserrat (1499), Madrid (1499), and perhaps Jaen (1500), complete the list of places where printing was practised in Spain before the end of the fifteenth century.

Numerous writers have asserted that printing began at Leiria in Estremadura as early as 1466. Antonio Ribeiro dos Santos, who wrote a learned dissertation on the subject, seems to place his chief reliance on a statement made by Pedro Affonso de Vasconcellos in 1588, that Leiria was the first town to receive the art; and on a further assertion by Soares de Silva, that he had seen a quarto volume containing the poems of the Infante Dom Pedro, which had at the end a note that it was printed nine years after the invention of printing. The particular copy here referred to was destroyed in 1755; other copies of the book contain no imprint. Whatever may be said about the probability of printing having been introduced at an early date into Portugal, the fact remains that the first authentic dated book appeared at Lisbon in 1489. It is a *Commentary on the Pentateuch*, by Moses ben Nachman, and was printed by two Jews, Rabbi Samuel Zorba and Rabbi Eliezer. It was through the Jews, shortly to be so ungratefully treated, that printing was introduced into two out of the three towns of Portugal in which it was practised in the fifteenth century. They were, however, a people apart, and the books which they printed were for their own use, and in a tongue not understood by others. It was not till 1495 that two other printers, Nicolaus de Saxonia and Valentinus de Moravia, started at Lisbon to issue books in other languages than Hebrew. Another Jew, Abraham, son of Don Samuel Dortas or de Orta, printed the earliest books of Leiria. The first book, the *Proverbs of Solomon*, with a commentary, was issued in 1492; and other books appeared in 1494 and 1496. The third and last town in Portugal where we find a printing press in the fifteenth century was Braga. Here, in 1494, a certain German named John Gherlinc, who seems to have printed later at Barcelona, printed a *Breviary* according to the use of the church of Braga. No other book is known to have been printed in this important town for the next forty years.

In the British Museum is a *Hebrew Pentateuch*, printed at 'Taro' in 1487. It is not known where this place was; but it has been conjectured that the name is a misprint for Faro, a town of Portugal (though it might stand for Toro in Leon); and if this is so, the date of the introduction of printing into Portugal must be placed two years farther back.

DENMARK AND SWEDEN.

The first book printed in Denmark, or indeed in the whole of the Northern countries, was an edition of *Gulielmi Caorsini de obsidione et bello Rhodiano*, of which a single copy is now preserved in the library at Upsala. It was printed in 1482 at Odensee, by John Snell, with the colophon: 'Per venerabilem virum Johannem Snel artis impressorie magistrum in Ottonia impressa sub anno domini 1482.' After the printing of this one book, Snell went to Stockholm. In 1486 one book was printed at Schleswig, by Stephen Arndes, who had already printed at Perusia, and who in 1487 appears at Lubeck. The book was the *Missale secundum Ordinarium et ritum Ecclesiæ Sleswicensis*, and no other was issued at this town in the fifteenth century. Next in order comes Copenhagen, to which, about 1490, Govaert van Ghemen moved from the Netherlands. The first dated book issued was the *Regulæ de figuratis constructionibus grammaticis* of 1493. According to M. Deschamps, this was preceded by a *Donatus*, without date, but having the name of the printer; and it is supposed that Govaert van Ghemen began to print in March 1490. He seems to have printed up to the year 1510.

John Snell, who has already been noticed as a printer at Odensee, came to Stockholm in 1483, and in that year printed the *Dialogus Creaturarum Moralizatus*, a small quarto of 156 leaves, with twenty-three lines to the page. [Hain, 6128.] Of this book four examples were known; one unfortunately perished in the fire at Abö in 1827. Of the others, two are at Upsala, and the third at Copenhagen. No other book appears at Stockholm until 1495, when the *Breviarium Strengenense* was printed. The printer's name is given as Johannes Fabri. And some writers would have this to be another form of the name Snell; Snell, they say, being the same 'practically' as Smed, Smed being our Smith, and

Faber or Fabri the Latin. This alteration, however, is not quite satisfactory.

In the same year as the *Breviarium Strengenense* was issued, the first book in Swedish was printed by the same printer. It is the *Bok af Djäfvulsens frästilse*, by John Gerson. The printer, John Fabri, died in the course of this year; for in the year following we find issued the *Breviarium secundum ritum ecclesiæ Upsalensis*, printed by the widow of John Fabri. One other book must be noticed as printed in the fifteenth century; it is the *De dignitate psalterii*, by Alanus de Rupe, printed probably at Stockholm, but with no printer's name. One book only is known to have been printed at Wadsten in the fifteenth century; it is an edition of the *Breviarium ad usum cœnobii Wadstenensis de ordine S. Brigittæ*, printed in 1495, an octavo with twelve lines to the page. Only one copy is known, which passed after the Reformation, with the rest of the books belonging to the monastery, into the library of Upsala. The printing press of this monastery came to an untimely end, for in the middle of October 1495 the whole of the part of the building where it stood was destroyed by fire. Of this occurrence an account is preserved; and we learn from it that not only did the monastery lose all its printing materials, but that a tub full of the *Revelaciones Sanctæ Brigittæ*, which had been printed in 1492 at Lubeck, by Bartholomæus Ghotan, and which the printer had sent up for sale, were also destroyed. Stockholm and Wadsten are the only places in Sweden where any books were produced in the fifteenth century; and the total number of books issued, according to Schröder's *Incunabula artis typographicæ in Suecia*, was six.

CHAPTER VIII.

THE history of the Introduction of Printing into England is comparatively clear and straightforward; for we have neither the difficulties of conflicting accounts, as in the case of Germany and the Low Countries, nor troublesome manuscript references which cannot be adequately explained, as in the case of France. Previous to 1477, when Caxton introduced the art in a perfect state, nothing had been produced in England but a few single sheet prints, such as the Images of Pity, of which there are copies in the British Museum and the Bodleian, and the cut of the Lion, the device of Bishop Gray (1454–1479), in Ely Cathedral.

There was no block-printing (for the verses on the seven virtues in the British Museum, and formerly in the Weigel Collection, are comparatively late), and with the one exception of the false date of 1468 in the first Oxford book, which we shall treat of later, there is nothing to confuse us in forming an absolutely clear idea of the introduction of the art into England, and its subsequent growth.

William Caxton, our first printer, was born, as he

himself tells us, 'in the Weald of Kent,' but unfortunately he has given us no clue to the date; probably it was about 1420; and in 1438 he was apprenticed to Robert Large, a mercer of the city of London, who was Lord Mayor in 1439–40. His business necessitated his residence abroad, and he doubtless left England shortly after his apprenticeship, for in 1469 he tells us that he had been 'thirty years for the most part in the countries of Brabant, Flanders, Holland, and Zetland.' In 1453 he visited England, and was admitted to the Livery of the Mercers' Company. About 1468 he was acting as governor to the 'English Nation residing abroad,' or 'Merchant Adventurers' at Bruges. After some six or seven years in this position, he entered the service of Margaret, Duchess of Burgundy, sister of Edward IV. The greater leisure which this appointment afforded him was employed in literary pursuits. In March 1469 he commenced a translation of the *Recueil des Histoires de Troyes*, by Raoul le Fèvre, but it was not finished till 19th September 1471, when Caxton was staying at Cologne.

This visit to Cologne marks an interesting period in Caxton's career, for it is most probable that it was there he learnt to print. Wynkyn de Worde tells us that the first book printed by Caxton was the *Bartholomæus de proprietatibus rerum*, and that it was printed at Cologne. It has been the general custom of writers to condemn this story as impossible, perhaps without sufficiently examining the facts.

spiritusáncto loquebátur
cum fiducia·testimoniũ·
R̃·Isti funt agni nouelli
qui annunciauerunt allã
mõ venerũt ad fontes re
pleti sũt claritate allã al
leluia·v̄·In cõspau agni
amicti stolis albis z pal
me in manib̃ coz·modo
R̃·Candidi·Et supr ad
vos·v̄·Vox leticie·In lau
dibus·añ·

Ancti tui dñe floze
bũt si aut lilium allã
et siaut odoz balsami erũt
añ te allã ps·Dñs regna
añ·Sãz iusti in domino
gaudete allã vos elegit d
us in hereditate sibi allã·
añ·In velamento clamãt
sacti tui domine allã allã
alleluia·añ·Spiritus et
anime iustozum ymnum
dicite deo nostro allã alle
luia añ·In celestibus eg
nis sanctoz habitacõ est
allã z ineternum requies
eozum allã Cap·ut sup
dictum est· Ymnus·
Vaxo paschali gau
dio sol mũdo nitet ra

dio cũ cristũ iam apostoli
visu cernunt corporeo·O
stensa sibi vulnea in cris
ti carne fulgida resurrex
isse dominũ vox fatentur
publica·Rex criste clemẽ
tissime tu cozda nrã possi
de ut tibi laudes debitas
reddamus omni tempore
Quesuus? auctoz·Glozia
tibi·v̄·Gaudete iusti in do
mino añ·Lux ppetua luce
bit scis tuis dñe allã z et
nitas tempoz allã allelu
ia allã ps Bñdaus·Ad p
añ Sã tui ps De? in no·
Ad iij añ·sancti z iusti
R̃·Tristicia vestra allã
alleluia v̄ Vertet i gaudi
um allã alleluia v̄ Precõ
sa est Ad vi añ·In vela
mento ps Deficit in salu
Cap ut supra R̃· Pretio
sa est in cõspau dñi all'a al
leluia v̄ Mors scoz eius
all'a v̄ Gaudete iusti Ad
ix añ·In celestilb ps Mi
rabilia Ca·ut õ R̃·Gau
dete iusti i dño all'a all'a
v̄ R̃·cõs dicet collaudacõ
al·glã·gaus v̄ Vox letf·

W. de Worde says in his preface to the English edition—

'And also of your charyte call to remembraunce
The soule of William Caxton the first prynter of this boke
In laten tongue at Coleyn, hymself to avaunce
That every well disposed man may thereon loke.'

Now, there is a Latin edition, evidently printed at Cologne about the time that Caxton was there, in a type almost identical with that of N. Gotz or the printer of the *Augustinus de fide;* and it was in conjunction with a very similar type, in 1476, that the 'gros bâtarde' type, which is so intimately connected with Caxton, first appeared. Though Caxton worked in partnership with Colard Mansion about 1475–77, he had probably learnt something of the art before ; and, taking into consideration his journey to Cologne, the statement of Wynkyn de Worde, and the typographical connexion between the *Bartholomæus* and Caxton's books, we may safely say that the story cannot be put aside as without foundation. It is not, of course, suggested that Caxton printed the book by himself, but only that he assisted in its production. He was learning the art of printing in the office where this book was being prepared, and his practical knowledge was acquired by assisting to print it.

Another Cologne book which may have been printed for Caxton, or produced through his means, is the first edition of the Breviary according to the use of Sarum. Unfortunately we only know of its

existence through a few leaves in the libraries at
Oxford, Cambridge, Lincoln, and Paris, and have
therefore no means of knowing by whom it was
printed, or whether it had any colophon at all. It
is a quarto, printed in two columns, and with thirty-
one lines to the column. Such a book would hardly
have been printed without the help of an English
stationer,—and who more likely than Caxton?

In 1477 an eventful change took place in Caxton's
career. 'On June 21, 1476, was fought the bloody
battle of Morat between the Duke of Burgundy and
the Swiss, which resulted in the ruin of the Burgundian
power. In the following January, the Duke, while
engaged in a murderous battle at Nanci, was over-
powered and fell, covered with wounds, stubbornly
fighting to the last. Caxton's mistress was now no
longer the ruling power at the court of Bruges. The
young daughter of the late Duke succeeded as the
reigning sovereign, and the Dowager Duchess of
Burgundy resigned her position at court, retiring into
comparative privacy on a handsome jointure. Caxton's
services as secretary would now be no longer required
by the Duchess in her altered position.'[1]

Early, therefore, in 1477, Caxton returned to
England, and set up his press in the Almonry at
Westminster. On 18th November of the same year
he finished printing the *Dictes or Sayengis of the
Philosophers*, the first book printed in England.
Copies of this book vary, some being without the

[1] *Who was Caxton?* By R. Hill Blades. London, 1877.

imprint. This was followed by an edition of the *Sarum Ordinale*, known now only from fragments, and the curious little 'cedula' relating to it, advertising the 'pyes of two or three commemorations.'

The productiveness of Caxton's press in its earliest years was most remarkable, for we know of at least thirty books printed within the first three years. A good many of these, however, were very small, the little tracts of Chaucer and Lydgate containing but a few leaves each. These were the 'small storyes and pamfletes' with which, according to Robert Copland, Caxton began his career as printer. On the other hand, we have the *History of Jason* (150 leaves), *The Canterbury Tales* (374 leaves), Chaucer's *Boethius* (94 leaves), the *Rhetorica Nova* of Laur: Gulielmus de Saona (124 leaves), the *Cordyal* (78 leaves), the second edition of the *Dictes or Sayengis* (76 leaves), and the *Chronicles of England* (182 leaves).

The starting of Lettou's press in London, in 1480, may probably account for some of the changes introduced by Caxton in that year. His first indulgence, printed this year in the large type, was at once thrown into the shade by the editions of the same indulgence issued by Lettou in his small neat letter, which was much better adapted for such work. Lettou also in this year used signatures, Caxton doing the same. The competition caused Caxton to make his fount of small type, and to introduce many other improvements. It was about this time that he introduced woodcuts into his books ; and the first book in which

I

we find them is the *Mirrour of the World.* The cuts
in this volume may be divided into two sets, those
given for the first time by Caxton, and those copied
from his predecessors. The first are ordinary woodcuts, the second what we should call diagrams. The
woodcuts are of the poorest design and coarsest execution. Several are of a master with four or five
pupils, others of single figures engaged in scientific
pursuits. The diagrams are more or less carefully
copied from the MSS.: they are numbered in the
table of contents as being eight in part I., nine in
part II., and ten [X. being misprinted for IX.] in
part III. Of the eight belonging to part I., Nos.
2 and 3 are put to their wrong chapters, and consequently No. 4 is omitted altogether. The diagrams
to part II. are wrongly drawn, and in some cases
misplaced. The nine diagrams to part III. are the
most correct. Some writers have contended that the
cuts in Caxton's books are from metal and not from
wood-blocks; but some of them which are found in
use at a considerably later date show marks of worm
holes, a conclusive proof of the material being wood.

To the year 1480 we can ascribe seven books, almost
all in the new type, No. 4. These are the French and
English phrase-book, Lidgate's *Curia Sapientiæ,* the
Chronicles of England, and the *Description of Britain;*
and three liturgical books, the *De Visitatione B.M.V.,*
the *Psalterium,* and a *Horæ ad usum Sarum,* the two
latter printed in type 3. Of the *Horæ,* but a few
leaves are known, which formed part of the won-

derful find of fragments in the binding of a copy of the *Boethius* at St. Albans Grammar School. This volume was found by Mr. Blades in 1858, and from the covers were taken no less than fifty-six half sheets of printed paper, proving the existence of three works from Caxton's press quite unknown before, the *Horæ* above mentioned, the *Ordinale*, and an indulgence of Pope Sixtus IV.

About 1481 appeared the first English edition of *Reynard the Fox;* and in that year two other books, both dated, *Tully of Old Age*, and the *Siege of Jerusalem.*

These were followed by the *Polycronicon*, the *Chronicles of England* (edit. 2), *Burgh's Cato*, and the second edition of the *Game of the Chesse*, which is illustrated with woodcuts, the first edition having none. There are altogether sixteen different woodcuts used in the volume, and eight occur twice.

Between 1483 and the end of 1485, Caxton was at his very busiest, issuing in that time about twenty-two books; and amongst them are some of the most important. There are the *Pilgrimage of the Soul*, the *Festial* and *Quattuor Sermones*, the *Sex Epistolæ*, of which the unique copy is now in the British Museum; the *Lyfe of Our Lady*, the second edition of the *Canterbury Tales* (the first with woodcuts), Chaucer's *Troilus and Cresida* and *Hous of Fame*, the *Confessio Amantis*, the *Knight of the Tower*, and *Æsop's Fables.* This book, which appeared 26th March 1484, has a full page frontispiece and no less than 185 woodcuts, the work of two, if not three, different cutters. They are of the very poorest execution, and not original in design, being more or less carefully copied from a foreign edition. The whole of the earlier part of 1485 must have been expended upon the production of the *Golden Legend*, the largest book which issued from Caxton's press. It contains 449 leaves, and is printed on a much larger sheet than was generally used by Caxton for folios, the full sheet measuring as much as 24 inches by 16 inches. It has, as illustrations, a large cut for the frontispiece, representing heaven, and two series of eighteen large and fifty-two small cuts, the large series including one of the device of the Earl of Arundel, to whom the book is dedicated. Most copies of the *Golden Legend* now in existence are made up partly of this and partly of the second edition. As far as can be judged, the distinguishing mark is the type of the headlines, which in the first edition are in type 3, and in the second edition in type 5. No copy is known made up entirely of one edition.

For the latter part of 1485 we have three dated books, the *Morte d'Arthur* (31st July), the only perfect copy of which is now, unfortunately, in America; the *Life of Charles the Great* (1st December), the only existing copy of which is in the British Museum; and *The Knight Paris and the Fair Vienne* (19th December), of which again the only known copy is in the British Museum.

In 1487, Caxton tried a new venture, and had printed for him at Paris, by George Maynyal, an edition of the *Sarum Missal.* Only one copy is known, slightly imperfect, which is in private hands. In this book, for the first time, Caxton used his well-known device, probably for the purpose of emphasising what might easily have been overlooked, —that the book was printed at his expense. So much has been written on Caxton's device, and such extraordinary theories made about its hidden meanings, that it may be as well to point out that it consists simply of his mark standing between his initials, with a certain amount of unmeaning ornament. It was probably cut in England, being coarsely executed, while those used in France at the same time are well cut and artistic. About 1487–88 we find two more books ornamented with woodcuts, the *Royal Book* and the *Speculum Vite Christi.* The *Speculum* contains a number of well-executed cuts, the *Royal Book* only seven, six of which had appeared in the *Speculum.*

About 1488 a second edition of the *Golden Legend* was issued, almost exactly the same as the first, but with the life of St. Erasmus added, so that this edition does not end, like the first, with a blank leaf. At the time of Caxton's death, he seems to have had a large stock of this book still on his hands, for he left fifteen copies to the Church of St. Margaret, and a large number of copies to his daughter Elizabeth, the wife of Gerard Croppe, a tailor in Westminster. It is hard to understand how, with this large stock still for sale, Wynkyn de Worde could afford to print a new edition in 1493 and another in 1498; for even at the latter date copies of Caxton's edition were, as we happen to know, still to be obtained.

To about this time may be ascribed the curious *Image of Pity* in the University Library, Cambridge. It is not printed on a separate piece of paper, but is a sort of proof struck off on the blank last page of a book with which the indulgence has nothing to do. The book is a copy of the *Colloquium peccatoris et Crucifixi J. C.*, printed at Antwerp by Mathias van der Goes about 1487, which must have been accidentally lying near when the printer wanted something to take an impression upon.[1]

In 1489, Caxton printed two editions of an indulgence of great typographical interest. This indulgence was first noticed by Dr. Cotton, who mentions it in his *Typographical Gazetteer* under Oxford, supposing it to have been printed at that place. Bradshaw, on seeing a photograph of it, at once conjectured from the form and appearance of the type that it was printed by Caxton, though Blades refused to accept it as a product of his press without further proof, and it was never admitted into any of his books on Caxton. The same type was afterwards found by Bradshaw used for sidenotes in the 1494 edition of

---

[1] For a detailed account of this and other English *Images of Pity*, see a paper by Henry Bradshaw, reprinted as No. 9 in his *Collected Papers*, p. 135.

the *Speculum Vite Christi*, printed by W. de Worde, and the type being in his possession at that date, could have belonged in 1489 to no one but Caxton.

In a list of Caxton's types this type would be known as type 7.

In addition to these two indulgences, a number of books may be assigned to this year. The *Fayttes of Arms* is dated ; but besides this there are the *Statutes of Henry VII.*, the *Governayle of Health*, the *Four Sons of Aymon*, *Blanchardyn and Eglantyne*, *Directorium Sacerdotum*, second edition, the third edition of the *Dictes or Sayengis*, the *Doctrinal of Sapience*, and an *Image of Pity* printed on one leaf. The second edition of *Reynard the Fox*, known only from the copy preserved in the Pepysian Library, may also be assigned to this year. With the exception of the *Eneydos*, the remainder of Caxton's books are of a religious or liturgical character. Amongst them we must class an edition probably of the *Horæ ad usum Sarum* not mentioned by Blades ; for though no copy or even fragment is now known, it is certain that such a book was printed. A set-off from a page of it was discovered by Bradshaw on a waste sheet of the *Fifteen Oes*. All that could be certainly distinguished was that it was printed in type 5, that there were twenty-two lines to a page, and that each page was surrounded by a border.

The *Fifteen Oes* itself is a most interesting book. It was printed originally, no doubt, as an extra part for an edition of the *Horæ ad usum Sarum* now entirely lost. It contains a beautifully executed woodcut of the crucifixion,—one of a series of five which occur complete in a *Horæ* printed by Wynkyn de Worde in 1494, and it is also the only existing book from this press which has borders to the pages. Caxton printed altogether about one hundred books, using in them altogether eight types. Blades gives ninety-nine books printed by Caxton, two of which were certainly printed by his associate in Bruges after Caxton had left for England. On the other hand, he does not mention the newly-discovered Grammar, the two editions of the Indulgence of 1489, a second edition of the *Lyf of our Lady*, known from a fragment in the Bodleian, and one or two other indulgences. One or two books which Blades includes were printed undoubtedly by De Worde, such as the *Book of Courtesye* (which, indeed, contains his small device), *The Chastysing of God's Children*, and the *Treatise of Love*. The genuine Caxtons catalogued by Blades number ninety-four.

As regards types, Blades gives six of Caxton's, and a seventh which he conjectures only to have been used by Wynkyn de Worde, though in this he was mistaken, for it occurs in books printed while Caxton was alive. Again, the type of the 1489 Indulgence which he does not mention, was conclusively proved by Bradshaw to be one of Caxton's types. This type should be considered as type 7, and the former type, which does not appear until 1490–91, as type 8. The woodcut initials which occur in the *Chastysing of God's Children* were not used till after Caxton's death.

But while we venerate Caxton as our first printer, we must not overlook the claims which he has upon us as a translator and editor. Wonderful as his diligence in press-work may appear, it is still more wonderful to consider how much literary work he found time to do in the intervals of his business. He was the editor of all the books which he printed, and he himself translated no less than twenty-two, including that great undertaking the *Golden Legend*. Even on his deathbed he was still at work, as we learn from the colophon of the *Vitas Patrum*, printed by Wynkyn de Worde in 1495 : ' Thus endyth the moost vertuouse hystorye of the deuoute and right renowned lyves of holy faders lyvynge in deserte, worthy of remembraunce to all wel dysposed persones, which hath ben translated oute of Frenche into Englysshe by William Caxton of Westmynstre late deed and fynysshed at the laste daye of hys lyff.'

On Caxton's death, in 1491, his materials passed into the hands of Wynkyn de Worde, his assistant, who continued to print in the same house at Westminster. Up to 1493 he continued to use Caxton's type, with the addition of some woodcut initials obtained from Godfried van Os, from whom he also obtained a complete set of type, which was not used till 1496, and then only for printing one book.

W. de Worde, though he must have lived for some time previously in England, only took out letters of denization in 1496. The grant is dated 20th April to 'Winando de Worde, de ducatu Lothoringie oriundo, impressori librorum.'

The earliest books which he printed have no name, and are all in Caxton's type, Nos. 6 and 4*, but with some additional types which distinguish his works from Caxton's.

From the time of Caxton's death, in 1491, to the time when his own name first appears in an imprint, Wynkyn de·Worde printed five books. They are the *Chastysing of God's Children*, the *Treatise of Love*, and the *Book of Courtesye*, all printed in type 6; and the *Golden Legend* and the *Life of St. Catherine*, printed in a modification of type 4*, a type which is used in no other books. The *Chastysing* is interesting as having a title-page, the first in any book from this office; while in the *Book of Courtesye* we find the device of W. de Worde used for the first time.

In 1493 we find for the first time a book containing De Worde's name. This is the *Liber Festivalis*, probably printed towards the end of the year, for the *Quattuor Sermones*, generally issued with it, is dated 1494. The next book to appear was Walter Hylton's *Scala Perfectionis;* and in the same year was issued a reprint of Bonaventura's *Speculum Vite Christi*, a book of very great interest, for the sidenotes are printed with the type which Caxton used for his Indulgence of 1489, and which was used for no other book than this. To this year 1494 we may ascribe a beautiful edition of the Sarum *Horæ*, adorned with

woodcuts and borders, nearly all of which were in-
herited from Caxton. The type which De Worde
used for these books seems to have come into Caxton's
hands from France, during the last year of his life,
and resembles closely certain founts which belonged
to the Paris printers P. Levet and Higman, if indeed
it is not the same. After 1494, De Worde discarded
it, using it only occasionally for headings or titles.
Blades wrongly says that the use of this type separ-
ates the early W. de Worde books from the Caxton's ;
but Caxton certainly possessed and used it. The
distinctive mark of the early Wynkyn de Worde
books is the use of the initials obtained from G. van
Os. Bradshaw, speaking of these, says, ' Indeed, the
woodcut initials are what specially serve at once to
distinguish W. de Worde's earliest from Caxton's
latest books.'

In 1495 we have three dated books, the *Vitas
Patrum*, which Caxton was engaged in translating up
to the day of his death ; Higden's *Polycronicon*, the
first English book containing musical notes, and
the *Directorium Sacerdotum*. Besides these, a fair
number of undated books may be ascribed to this
year or the year after. The most important is the
Bartholomæus, *De Proprietatibus Rerum*. Apart
from its ordinary interest, it is considered to be the
first book printed on paper made in England.

' And John Tate the younger, joye mote he broke,
Whiche late hath in Englond doo made this paper thynne
That now in our englisshe this boke is prynted Inne.'

In 1496 appeared the curious reprint of the *Book of St. Albans*. It seems never to have been noticed that this book is entirely printed with the type which was obtained from Godfried van Os about the time of his removal to Copenhagen. Besides the *Book of St. Albans*, it has an extra chapter on fishing with an angle, the first treatise on the subject in English. An edition of the *Dives and Pauper*, with a handsome title-page, was issued this year, as well as a number of smaller books of considerable interest, as the *Constitutions* of Lyndewode, the *Meditacions* of St. Bernard, and the *Festial* and *Quattuor Sermones*. Among the dated books of 1497 are the *Chronicles of England*, an edition copied from the one printed at St. Albans; and it is from the colophon to this edition that we learn that the printer at St. Albans was ' sometyme scole mayster' there.

In 1498 three large and important books were printed ; of these the first was an edition of the *Golden Legend*, of which only one perfect copy is known, in the Spencer Collection; the next, a second edition of the *Morte d'Arthur*, the first illustrated with wood-cuts. The only known copy of this book, wanting ten leaves, is also in the Spencer Library. The third book was an edition of the *Canterbury Tales*. In 1499 a large number of books were printed, the most curious being an edition of *Mandeville's Travels*, illustrated profusely with woodcuts of the wonders seen by the traveller, who got as far as the walls of Paradise, but did not look in. Of this book two copies, both imperfect, are known. A *Book of Good Manners* and a *Psalterium*, both known from single copies, were also printed in this year. An *Ortus Vocabulorum*, printed in 1500, is the last book which was issued by De Worde at Westminster. Altogether, from 1491 to the time he left Caxton's old house at Westminster, W. de Worde printed about a hundred books, certainly not less; and he also had a few books printed for him, and at his expense, by other printers.

In a very large number of De Worde's early books he inserted the cut of the crucifixion, which is first found in Caxton's *XV Oes*. In 1499 the block split at the time when they were printing an edition of the *Mirror of Consolation*, sometime after the 10th July, so that all the books which contain the cut in its injured state must be later than 10th July 1499.

The year 1500 gives us an excellent date-mark for W. de Worde's books, for in that year he moved from Westminster 'in Caxton's house,' to London, in Fleet Street, at the sign of the Sun. Upon moving he seems to have destroyed or disposed of a good deal of printing material. Some of his woodcuts passed to Julian Notary, who was also at that time a printer in Westminster. One of his marks and some of his type disappear entirely at this time. The type which he had used in the majority of the books printed in the last few years of the fifteenth century we find in use up to 1508 or 1509, when it disappears from London to reappear at York; but his capitals and

marks had changed. From 1504 onward he used in
the majority of his books the well-known square
device in three divisions, having in the upper part the
sun and moon and a number of stars. In the centre
the W. and C. and Caxton's mark; below this the
'Sagittarius' shooting an arrow at a dog. It has not
hitherto been noticed that of this device there are
three varieties, identical to a superficial view, yet
quite distinct and definitely marking certain periods.
The first variety in use from 1505 to 1518 has in the
upper part eleven stars to the left of the sun and
nine to the right, while the white circular inlets at
the ends of the W. are almost closed. The second
variety used from 1519 to the middle of 1528 has the
same number of stars, but the circular inlets at the
ends of the letters are more open. The last variety
has ten stars to the left of the sun and ten to the right.
It was used from 1528 to the time of De Worde's
death. In the colophons of some of his early books
De Worde mentions that he had another shop in St.
Paul's Churchyard, with the sign of Our Lady of
Pity.

Wynkyn de Worde was essentially a popular
printer, and he issued innumerable small tracts;
short romances in prose and verse, books of riddles,
books on carving and manners at table, almanacs,
sermons, grammars, and such like. Many of these
books were translations from the French, and were
made by Robert Copland, who was one of De
Worde's apprentices. The later books of De Worde

are often puzzling. He seems to have employed John Scot to print for him, and many books which have only De Worde's name are in Scot's type. One book is particularly curious. It is an edition of *The Mirror of Golde for the Sinful Soul*, 29th March 1522. Some copies have a colophon, 'Imprinted at London withoute Newgate, in Saint Pulker's Parysche, by John Scot.' Other copies have the first sheet and the last leaf reset, while the colophon runs, 'Imprinted at London in Fletestrete, at the sygne of the Sone, by Wynkyn de Worde.'

De Worde died at the end of 1534. His will is dated 5th June 1534, and it was proved 19th January 1535. His executors were John Bedill, who succeeded him in business, and James Gaver, probably a bookbinder, and one of the numerous family of that name who exercised their craft in the Low Countries. In the forty years that he printed, Wynkyn de Worde produced over six hundred books, that is, more than fifteen a year, a much higher average than any other early English printer attained.

About the year 1496 three printers started in partnership at the sign of St. Thomas the Apostle in London. They were Julian Notary, Jean Barbier, and a third whose name is not known, but whose initials were I. H., and who may perhaps have been Jean Huvin. The first book which they printed was the *Questiones Alberti de modis significandi*, a quarto of sixty leaves, printed in a clear, handsome black letter. At the end of the book is a printer's mark, with the initials of the printers, but there is no colophon to tell us either their names or the date of printing. In 1497 they issued an edition of the *Horæ ad usum Sarum*, printed, as we learn from the colophon, for Wynkyn de Worde. The same printer's mark is in this book, but again we have no information about the names of the printers. In 1498 the firm had changed.,—I. H. had left, and the two remaining printers, Notary and Barbier, had moved to Westminster, perhaps in order to be nearer the printer for whom they worked. In this year they printed an edition of the *Sarum Missal* for Wynkyn de Worde, and after this Jean Barbier returns to France, leaving Notary at Westminster by himself. There he continued to print up to some time before 1503, and in that year we find him living 'without Temple Bar, in St. Clement's Parish, at the sign of the Three Kings.' Before moving, he had printed, besides the books mentioned above, a *Festial* and *Quattuor Sermones* in 1499, a *Horæ ad usum Sarum* in 1500, and the Chaucer's *Complaint of Mars and Venus*, without date. About this time he obtained some woodcuts from Wynkyn de Worde, and we find them used in the first book he printed at his new address, the *Golden Legend* of 1503[4], and in it also are to be found some very curious metal cuts in the 'manière criblée.' An undated *Sarum Horæ*, in which the calendar begins with 1503, should most probably be put before the *Golden Legend*. From 1504 to 1510 Notary printed about

¶ Here begynneth nexte the Ascensyon of our lozde.

The ascensyon of oure lozde Jhesu cryste was to fourty day after hys resurreccyon. For whyche too declare: seuen thynges ben to be consydered. Fyrst thene he ascended. Secondly why he ascended anone after hys Resurreccyon Thirdly how he ascēded Fourthly what compa‧ ny ascended wyth hym. Fyfthly by what merite he ascended Syxtly whe re he ascended. And seuently wherfoze he ascended.

¶ As too the fyrst he ascended fro the mount of oly‧ uete by bethanye The whyche mountayn after a no ter relacyon/is sayd the mountayne of thze lyghtes.

¶ For by nyghte oon the syde of the weste it is ly‧ ghtedde of the fyree / that bzennethe in the tem‧ ple. whyche neuer is put out nequenched. On the mozynge it is lyght of thozpent / foz she hathe fyrste the rapes of the sonne/befoze it shyneth in the cytee. And also it hathe grete haboundaunce of oyle that nozyssheth the lyghte. and therfoze it is sayde the hil

Li

thirteen books, and in that latter year (as we learn from the imprint of the *Expositio Hymnorum*) he had, besides his shop without Temple Bar, another in St. Paul's Churchyard, of which the sign was also the Three Kings.

Between 1510 and 1515, Notary issued no dated book, but in the latter year appeared the *Chronicles of England*, and in the year following two *Grammars* of Whittington. The old printing-office 'Extra Temple Bar' seems to have been given up, for at this time Notary was printing in Paul's Churchyard, at the sign of St. Mark. After 1515 there is another interval of three years without a dated book ; but between 1518 and 1520 several were issued from the sign of the Three Kings in Paul's Churchyard, and after that Notary printed no more. His movements from place to place are difficult to understand. In 1497 he is in London at the sign of St. Thomas Apostle, in 1498 at Westminster in King Street. About 1502–3 he moves to a house outside Temple Bar, the one probably that Pynson had just vacated. In 1510, while still printing at the same place, he had a shop in St. Paul's Churchyard at the sign of the Three Kings. In 1515 he is at the sign of St. Mark in Paul's Churchyard, in 1518 again at the Three Kings. It seems probable that some of his productions must have entirely disappeared, otherwise it is hard to account for the number of blank years.

The latest writer on Julian Notary conjectures that

K

the sign of St. Mark and the sign of the Three Kings
were attached to the same house; that Julian Notary,
on moving to Paul's Churchyard, went to a house
with the sign of St. Mark, and after printing under
that sign for two years, altered it, for commercial
reasons, to his old emblem of the Three Kings.
This is ingenious, but impossible, for the writer has
ignored the fact that Notary had a shop in St. Paul's
Churchyard at the Three Kings five years before we
hear of the one with the sign of St. Mark.

CHAPTER IX.

As early as 1664, when Richard Atkyns issued his *Original and Growth of Printing*, the assertion was put forward that printing in England was first practised at Oxford. ' A book came into my hands,' says Atkyns, 'printed at Oxon, Anno Dom. 1468, which was three years before any of the recited Authours would allow it to be in England.'

The book here referred to is the celebrated *Exposicio sancti Jeronimi in simbolum apostolorum*, written by Tyrannius Rufinus of Aquileia ; and in the colophon it is clearly stated that the book was printed in 1468. 'Impressa Oxonie et finita anno domini .M. cccc. lxviij xvij. die decembris.'

Many writers have argued for and against the authenticity of the date; and though some are still found who believe in its correctness, it is generally allowed to be a misprint for 1478. In the first place, the book has printed signatures, which have not been found in any book before 1472. Again, copies of this book have been found bound up in the original binding with books of 1478. In the library of All Souls College, Oxford, is a copy bound up with one of the

1479 books, and though the present binding is modern, they were originally bound together; and we find a set-off from the damp ink of the second volume on the last leaf of the first. A copy in another Oxford library, bound up with the 1479 books, has been marked for or by the binder with consecutive signatures all through the several tracts. Instances of misprinted dates are far from rare. The *Matara-tius de componendis versibus*, printed at Venice by Ratdolt, is dated 1468 instead of 1478, and was on that account sometimes put forward as a proof of early printing there. Spain, too, claimed printing for the same year on account of a misprinted ' 1468 ' in a grammar printed at Barcelona. A *Vocabularius rerum*, printed by John Keller at Augsburg, has the same misprint of 1468. However, the surest test of the date of a book is to place it alongside others from the same press, and compare the workmanship. In this case the book falls naturally into its place at the head of the Oxford list in 1478, taking just the small precedence of the two books of 1479, which the slightly lesser excellence of its workmanship warrants. A break of eleven years between two books which are in every way so closely allied would be almost impossible, and quite unsupported by other instances. Accepting 1478 as the correct date, it is clear that Oxford lost no time in employing the new art, for Caxton had only commenced at Westminster the year before.

The first three books, the *Exposicio* of 1478 before

mentioned, and the *Ægidius de originali peccato*, and *Textus ethicorum Aristotelis per Leonardum Aretinum translatus*, both of 1479, form a group of themselves. They are printed in a type either brought from Cologne or directly copied from Cologne work, and strongly resembling that used by Gerard ten Raem de Berka or Guldenschaff. None have a printer's name, but they are ascribed to Theodore Rood of Cologne, the printer of the other early Oxford books.

The earliest of these three, the *Exposicio*, is a small quarto of forty-two leaves, with twenty-five lines to the page, and the other two are generally similar in type and form. There are, however, one or two differences to be noted in it. The edges on the right-hand margin are often uneven, the letters Q, H, g are often wrongly used, the text begins on A1 instead of on the second leaf, and it was printed one page at a time. These faults were all rectified in the two later books, which leave little to be desired in the way of execution.

The next dated book appeared in 1481, and it has the advantage of a full colophon giving the name of the printer. It is a Latin commentary on the *De Animâ* of Aristotle, by Alexander de Hales; a folio of 240 leaves, printed in type which had not been used before,—a curious, narrow, upright Gothic, not unlike in general appearance some of the founts used at Zwoll, or by Ther Hoernen at Cologne. A copy of this book was bought in the year that it was published

for the library of Magdalen College, Oxford, where it
still remains, for the sum of thirty-three shillings and
fourpence. In 1482 was issued a *Commentary on the
Lamentations of Jeremiah*, by John Lattebury, a folio
of 292 leaves. This is one of the least rare of the
early Oxford books, and three copies of it are known
printed upon vellum. The most interesting of these
is in the library of All Souls College, Oxford. It is
a beautiful copy in the original Oxford binding, and
the various quires are signed by the proof-readers.
Shortly after the issue of the *Lattebury*, the press
acquired an extremely beautiful woodcut border, and
the copies still remaining in stock of the *Lattebury*
and the *Alexander de Hales* were rendered more
attractive by having this border printed round the
first page of text, and at the beginning of some of
the divisions. In this second issue of the two books,
some sheets also appear to have been reprinted.

With these two books may be classed two others,
in both cases known only from fragments, an edition
of *Cicero pro Milone* and a Latin Grammar. The
Cicero pro Milone is a quarto, and would have contained about thirty leaves. At present only eight
leaves are known ; four in the Bodleian, and four in
Merton College Library. This was the first edition
of a classic printed in England. Of the Latin
Grammar only two leaves are known, which are in
the British Museum.

The third and last group contains eight books, of
which only one contains a printer's name. This is

found in the colophon to the *Phalaris* of 1485, a
curious production in verse running as follows :—

> ' Hoc Teodericus rood quem collonia misit
>   Sanguine germanus nobile pressit opus
>   Atque sibi socius thomas fuit anglicus hunte.
>   Dij dent ut venetos exuperare queant
>   Quam ienson venetos decuit vir gallicus artem
>   Ingenio didicit terra britanna suo
>   Celatos veneti nobis transmittere libros
>   Cedite nos alijs vendimus o veneti
>   Que fuerat vobis ars primum nota latini
>   Est eadem nobis ipsa reperta patres
>   Quamvis semotos toto canit orbe britannos
>   Virgilius. placet his lingua latina tamen.'

From this we learn that Rood had taken as his
partner one Thomas Hunt, an Englishman, who had
been established as a stationer in Oxford as early as
1473. He was probably associated with Rood in the
production of all the books in the last group, and his
influence may be perhaps traced in the new founts of
type used in them, which are much more English in
appearance than any which had been used at this
press before.

One of the earliest of the books of this last group
is the Latin Grammar by John Anwykyll, with the
Vulgaria Terencii. Of the first part, the Grammar,
which contained about 128 leaves, only one imperfect
copy, now in the Bodleian, is known. Of the other
part, the *Vulgaria*, at least four copies are known,
and an inscription on the copy belonging to the
Bodleian gives us a clue to the date. On its first

leaf is written the following inscription : — ' 1483.
Frater Johannes Grene emit hunc librum Oxonie de
elemosinis amicorum suorum '—Brother John Grene
bought this book at Oxford with the gifts of his
friends. 1483 is, then, the latest date to which we can
ascribe the printing of the book ; and this fits it into
its place, after the books of 1481 and 1482 printed in
the earlier type.

After the *Anwykyll* comes a book by Richard
Rolle of Hampole, *Explanationes super lectiones beati
Job*, a quarto of sixty-four leaves, of which all the three
known copies are in the University Library, Cambridge. With this may be classed a unique book in
the British Museum, a sermon of Augustine, *Excitatio
ad elemosinam faciendam*, a quarto of eight leaves.
This book, bound with five other rare tracts, was lot
4912 in the Colbert sale, and brought the large price
of 1 livre, 10 sous, about half-a-crown in our money.
Another quarto, similar to the last two, follows, a
collection of treatises on logical subjects, usually
associated with the name of Roger Swyneshede, who
was most probably the author of one only out of the
nineteen different parts. It is a quarto of 164 leaves,
and the only perfect copy known is in the library of
New College, Oxford ; another copy, slightly imperfect, being in the library of Merton College.

Next in our conjectural arrangement comes the
Lyndewode, *Super constitutiones provinciales*, a large
folio of 366 leaves. This is the first edition of the
celebrated commentary of William Lyndewode, and

Excitacio fidelis anime ad ele ʒ
mosinam faciendam A bt̄o Au⸗
gustino conscripta.

N lectione saucti euange
hj hortatus est nos dn̄s ad orādū
Petite inquit ꝭ dabitur uobis .
querite ꝭ inue nietis . Pulsate ꝭ
apietur uobis . Omnis em̄ qui
petit accipit.ꝭ querens inueniet ꝭ pulsanti ape
rietur. Aut quis est ex uobis homo a quo petit
filius eius pane.nūquid lapidem porriget illi .
Aut si piscem petierit.nūquid serpentem porri⸗
git ei.Aut cū petit ouū.scorpionem porrigit ei
Si ergo uos inquit cū sitis mali. nostis bona
data dare filijs uestris. quanto magis pr̄ us ʒ
ster qui ī celis .dabit bona petentibus se.Cum
sitis inquit mali: nostis bona data dare filijs
uestris. Miranda res fratres.Mali sumus bo
nū patrem habemus.Quid euidentius.Audi⸗
nimus nomen n̄r̄i . Cū sitis inquit mali. bo
na dare nostis filijs uestris. Et quos dixit
malos.Dicite quale patre illis ostendit Qua
to magis pater uester. Quorum pater. Certe
malorū.Et qualis pater.Nemo bonus:nisi so
lus deus . Ergo fres.ideo mali bonū patrem
habemus:ne semper mali remaneamus.Nemo
q̄ ij

of the Provincial Constitutions of England. On the verso of the first leaf is a woodcut, the first occurring in an Oxford book.

Ascribed to the year 1485 are the *Doctrinale* of Alexander Gallus and the Latin translation of the *Epistles of Phalaris*, whose colophon has been already noticed.

The *Doctrinale* of Alexander Gallus is known only from two leaves in the library of St. John's College, Cambridge. These leaves are used as end papers in the binding of a book; and a volume in the library of Corpus Christi College, Cambridge, bound in identically the same manner, has also as end papers two leaves of an Oxford printed book. That these two books must have been bound by the same man, almost at the same time, is shown from the fact that in both we find used vellum leaves from one and the same manuscript along with the refuse Oxford leaves.

The Latin translation of the *Epistles of Phalaris*, by Franciscus Aretinus, is in many ways the most interesting of this last group of Oxford books, containing as it does a very full colophon. It was printed, so the colophon tells us, in the 297th Olympiad, which those who write on the subject say was the year 1485. It is a quarto of eighty-eight leaves, and a very fine perfect copy is in the library of Wadham College, Oxford; two other copies are known, belonging to Corpus Christi College, Oxford, and the Spencer Library.

The last book issued by the Oxford press was the

Liber Festialis, a book of sermons for the holy days, by John Mirk. Several imperfect copies of this book are known, the most complete being in the library of Lambeth Palace. It is a folio of 174 leaves, and contains a series of eleven large cuts and five small ones. This series of large cuts (together with the cut of an author at work on his book, which occurs in the *Lyndewode*, and which is clearly one of the set), were not cut for the *Festial*, but appear to have been prepared for some edition of the *Golden Legend*. It was to have been a large folio book, for when we find the cuts used in the *Festial*, they have been cut at one end to allow them to fit the smaller sized sheet.

The *Festial* is dated 1486, but has no printer's name. After this we know of no other book produced in Oxford during the fifteenth century, and we have no information to account for the cessation of the press. It is possible, however, that Rood left Oxford and returned to Cologne. Panzer (vol. iv. p. 274) mentions two books, *Questiones Aristotelis de generatione et corruptione* and *Tres libri de anima Aristotelis*, printed at Cologne by a printer named Theodoricus in 1485 and 1486. In the library at Munich is a copy of the first book, and a facsimile of a page was published lately in Burger's *Monumenta Germaniæ et Italiæ Typographica*.

Now the type in which this book is printed bears the very strongest resemblance in many respects to that used by Rood at Oxford in 1481 and 1482, and the similarity of the names makes it possible, if not probable, that Rood was the printer. The *Questiones Aristotelis de generatione et corruptione* was finished at Cologne, 'anno incarnationis dominice 1485 in vigilia S. Andreæ apostoli per Theodoricum impressorem colonie infra sedecim domos.'[1]

The vigil of St. Andrew was the 29th of November, so that Rood had not much time to move from Oxford and start his new office between the date of the publication of the *Phalaris*, 1485, and the 29th of November of the same year.

Ennen and Madden consider that this Theodoricus was a certain Theodoric de Berse, whose name occurs in a list of printers and stationers of Cologne in 1501.

It is impossible with our present knowledge to say any more on the question; but if Rood did return to Cologne, the *Festial* must have been printed by Hunt alone. With it the fifteenth century printing at Oxford suddenly ceased, after a fairly prosperous career of eight years, during which at least fifteen books were issued.

From 1486 onward we have no further record of printing there till the year 1517. In the meanwhile the stationers supplied such books as were required; and to some of them we find incidental references, both in accounts and in the colophons of books printed for them.

---

[1] At this same address, where, in 1470, Ther Hoernen was living, we afterwards find John Landen. It is not, however, quite clear that 'infra sedecim domos' was the denomination of a particular house.

In 1506, Pynson printed an edition of the *Principia* of Peregrinus de Lugo, at the expense of Georgius Castellanus, who was living at the sign of St. John the Evangelist.   Between 1512 and 1514, Henry Jacobi, a London stationer, moved to Oxford, and started business at the sign of the Trinity, the sign which he had used when in London.   He died at Oxford in 1514.   In 1517 the new press was started by John Scolar, who lived 'in viculo diui Joannis baptiste.'   The first book he issued was a commentary by Walter Burley on a part of Aristotle, and this was followed in the next year by another book by the same author, *De materia et forma*.   In 1518 were also issued the *Questiones super libros ethicorum*, by John Dedicus [15 May], the *Compendium questionum de luce et lumine* [5 June], and Robert Whitinton's *De heteroclitis nominibus* [27 June].   To the same year may be assigned a *Prognostication* by Jasper Laet, of which there is a copy in the Cambridge University Library.   In 1519 there is only one book, printed by a new man, for Scolar has disappeared.   It is the *Compotus manualis ad usum Oxoniensium*, printed by Charles Kyrfoth, who lived like Scolar 'in vico diui Joannis baptiste,' and perhaps succeeded the latter in business.   From this time forward no books were printed in Oxford till 1585, when the University Press was started by Joseph Barnes, and commenced its career by issuing the *Speculum moralium quæstionum* of John Case.

One more early Oxford stationer must be mentioned

as connected with printing, and this is John Dorne or
Thorne, who was in business about 1520, and whose
most interesting Day-book was edited some years ago
by Mr. Falconer Madan for the Oxford Historical
Society. He was originally a stationer, and perhaps
printer, at Brunswick. A small educational work, the
*Opusculum insolubilium secundum usum insignis scole
paruisi in alma universitate Oxonie*, printed by
Treveris, was to be sold 'apud I. T.' These initials
stand probably for John Thorne, and we find the
book mentioned in his accounts.

ST. ALBAN'S.

The schoolmaster printer of St. Alban's has left us
no information as to his life, or even told us his
name, and we should know nothing whatever about
him had not W. de Worde referred to him as
'sometime schoolmaster of St. Albans.'

The press was probably started in 1479; for though
the earliest dated book is dated 1480, an edition from
this press of *Augustini Dacti elegancie*, in quarto, is
evidently earlier, being printed throughout in one
type, the first of those used by this printer. Of this
book one copy only is known, in the University
Library, Cambridge.

In 1480 the schoolmaster printer issued the *Rhetorica Nova* of Laurentius de Saona, a book which
Caxton was printing about the same time, and very
soon after it the *Questiones Alberti de modo significandi*.

These were followed by three more works in Latin, the *Questiones super Physica Aristotelis* of Joannes Canonicus, the *Exempla Sacræ Scripturæ,* and Antonius Andreæ *super Logica Aristotelis.* The remaining two books from this press, in contrast to those that had preceded them, are of a popular character. These are the *Chronicles of England,* and the treatise on hawking, hunting, and coat armour, commonly known as the *Book of St. Alban's.*

All the eight St. Alban's books are of the greatest rarity. More than half are known only from single copies; of some, not a single perfect copy remains.

The very scholastic nature of the majority of the books from this press renders it more or less uninteresting; but the two latest works, the *Chronicles* and the *Book of St. Alban's,* appeal more to popular taste. Editions of the *Chronicles* were issued by every English printer, and there is nothing in this particular one to merit special remark. The *Book of St. Alban's,* on the other hand, is a book of very particular interest. It consists of three parts; the first is devoted to hawking, the second to hunting, and the third to coat armours or heraldry. Naturally enough it was a popular book—so popular that no perfect copy now exists. It also possesses the distinction of being the first English book which contains specimens of printing in colour; for the coats-of-arms at the end are for the most part printed in their correct colour. Later in the century, in 1496, W. de Worde

issued another edition of this book, adding to it a
chapter on 'Fishing with an angle.'

In these eight St. Alban's books we find four
different types used. The first is a small, clear-cut,
distinctive type, but is only used for the text of
one book and the signatures of others. Type
No. 2, which is used for the text of the two English
and one of the Latin books, is a larger ragged
type, with a strong superficial resemblance to
Caxton's. Type No. 3, which is used in four Latin
books, is a smaller type, full of abbrevations and
contractions; while the last type is one which had
belonged to Caxton (his type 3), but which he
gave up using about 1484. This use of Caxton's
type has led some people to imagine that there was
a close connection between the Westminster and
St. Alban's press; and a writer in the *Athenæum*
went so far as to propound a theory that Caxton's
unsigned books were really printed at St. Alban's.

CHAPTER X.

LONDON.

John Lettou, William de Machlinia, Richard Pynson.

IN 1480, printing was introduced into London by John Lettou, perhaps a native of Lithuania, of which Lettou is an old form. The first product of the press was an edition of John Kendale's Indulgence asking for aid against the Turks, another edition having just been issued by Caxton in his large No. 2* type. As we have said, Lettou's small neat type was very much better suited for printing indulgences, and its appearance very probably caused Caxton to make his small type No. 4, which he used in future for such work. Besides two other editions of the indulgence, Lettou printed only one book in this year, the *Quæstiones Antonii Andreæ super duodecim libros metaphysice Aristotelis.* It is a small folio of 106 leaves, of very great rarity, only one perfect copy being known, in the library of Sion College, London. In 1481 another folio book was printed, *Thomas Wallensis super Psalterium,* and probably in the same year a work on ecclesiastical procedure, known only from two leaves which were found in the binding of one of the Parker books in Corpus Christi College, Cambridge.

From the workmanship of these books we can clearly see that Lettou was a practised printer, though we know nothing as to where he learnt his art. His type, which bears no resemblance to any other used in England, is very similar to that of Matthias Moravus, the Naples printer; so similar, indeed, as to make it certain that there must have been some connexion between the two printers, or some common origin for their types. Lettou was assisted by a certain William Wilcock, at whose expense the two large books were printed.

About 1482, Lettou was joined by another printer, William de Machlinia, a native no doubt of Malines in Belgium. These two printers employed a new fount of type of the same school as the other English types, and one suitable for the printing of the law-books, which were their sole productions. In partnership they printed but five books, the *Tenores Novelli*, the *Abridgment of the Statutes*, and the *Year-Books* of the 33rd, 35th, and 36th years of Henry VII. The first of these books is the only one which has a colophon. It gives the names of the two printers, and states that the book was printed in the city of London, 'juxta ecclesiam omnium sanctorum;' a rather vague address, since, according to Arnold's Chronicle, there were several London churches thus dedicated.

After these books had been issued, about 1483–84, John Lettou disappears, and Machlinia carried on his business alone. By himself he printed at least twenty-two books or editions. Out of all this number only four contain his name, and not one a date. He printed at two addresses, 'By Flete-brigge,' and in Holborn. If these two addresses refer to two different places, and we have no reason for supposing the contrary, there is no doubt that 'By Flete-brigge' is the earlier.

How late he continued to carry on business it is not possible to find out, as none of his books are dated. The Bull of Innocent VIII., relating to the marriage of Henry VII., which he printed, cannot have been issued till after 2nd March 1486; and the occurrence of a title-page in one of his books points to a still later date, for we know of no other book having a title-page printed in England before 1491–92.

Machlinia's use of signatures and initial directors seems to have been entirely arbitrary, and it is impossible to arrange the books in any certain order from their typographical peculiarities.

In the 'Flete-brigge' type there are nine books. Two works of Albertus Magnus, the *Liber aggregationis* and the *De secretis mulierum;*[1] a *Horæ ad usum Sarum*, known only from fragments rescued from old bindings; the *Revelation of St. Nicholas to a monk of Evesham*, of which the two known copies show curious instances of wrong imposition. There are,

---

[1] The copy of this book in the University Library, Cambridge, wanting all signature *c*, but in fine condition, and uncut, has on the first blank leaf some early writing which refers to the year 1485, showing probably that the book was not printed after that date.

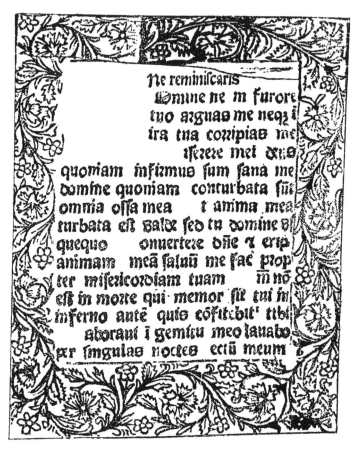

ne reminiscaris

Dmine ne m furore
tuo arguas me neqʒ i
ira tua corripias me
iserere mei due
quoniam infirmus sum sana me
domine quoniam conturbata sū
omnia ossa mea t anima mea
turbata est valde sed tu domine ō
quequo onuertere dñe t erip
animam meā saluū me fac prop
ter misericordiam tuam m nō
est in morte qui memor sit tui in
inferno autē quis cōfitebit tibi
aboraui i gemitu meo lauabo
per singulas noctes lectū meum

PAGE OF THE SARUM HORÆ.

(Printed by Machlinia.)

besides, three law - books and a school - book, the *Vulgaria Terencii.* Of the *Horæ ad usum Sarum* twenty leaves are known, all printed on vellum. In size it might be called a 16mo, and was made up in gatherings of eight leaves, each gathering containing two sheets of vellum. These gatherings were folded in a peculiar way. As an ordinary rule, when we find a quire of eight leaves formed of two sheets, leaves 1, 2, 7, 8 were printed on one sheet, leaves 3, 4, 5, 6 on the other. But Machlinia adopted a different plan, and printed leaves 1, 4, 5, 8 on the one sheet, leaves 2, 3, 6, 7 on the other. It is impossible to say whether there were any cuts in the volume; there are none in the remaining fragments, but at the beginning of certain portions a woodcut border was used, which surrounded the whole page. This border was afterwards used by Pynson. A curious thing to be noticed about the type in which these books are printed, is its very strong resemblance to some of the founts of type used about the same period in Spain.

In the Holborn type there are a larger number of books, at least fourteen being known. Of these the best known and most common is the *Speculum Christiani*, supposed, from the occurrence of the name in a manuscript copy, to have been compiled by one Watton. It is interesting as containing specimens of early poetry. Another book was popular enough to run through three editions; this was the *Treatise on the Pestilence*, written by Kamitus or Canutus, bishop of Aarhuus. It is impossible to say when it was printed, or whether some panic connected with the plague caused a run upon it. One of the editions must have been almost the last book which Machlinia issued, for it contains the title-page already referred to. The most important book in this set in point of size is the *Chronicles of England*, of which only one perfect copy is known. In the copy in the British Museum occurs a curious thing. The book is a folio, but two of the leaves are printed as quarto. In this type are three law-books, *Year-Books* for years 34 and 37 of Henry VI., and the *Statutes* of Richard III. There are also two school-books, the *Vulgaria Terentii* and an interesting *Donatus* in folio, whose existence is known only from duplicate copies of one leaf. The remaining books are theological, and comprise two separate *Nova Festa*, or services for new feasts ; one for the Visitation of the Virgin, the other for the Transfiguration of our Lord. These services were almost at once incorporated in the general volume of the *Breviary*, so that in a separate form they are very uncommon. The last book to be mentioned is the *Regulæ et ordinationes* of Innocent VIII., which must have been printed some time after 23rd September 1484, when that pope was elected. Of a later date still is a *Bull* of the same pope relating to Henry VII.'s title and marriage. It must have been printed after 7th November 1485 (the date of Parliament), and after 2nd March 1485–86 (the date of the *Bull*).

Another book should be mentioned here, which,

though it cannot with certainty be ascribed to any known English printer, resembles most of all the work of Machlinia. It is an English translation by Kay of the Latin description of the *Siege of Rhodes*, written by Caorsin ; a small folio of twenty-four leaves. Many of the letters seem the same as Machlinia's, but with variations and modifications.

The number of founts of type used in this office throughout its existence was eleven, and of these two are very peculiar. One of the larger sets of type seems to have been obtained from Caxton, but it was hardly used at all. Another set of capital letters, which must have been obtained from abroad, occur in some of the latest books. They bear no resemblance to anything used by any other printer, and look rather as though they belonged to a fount of Roman type.

Though 1486 is the latest date which we can fix to any of Machlinia's productions, it is probable that he continued to print up till about the year 1490.

Soon after the cessation of Machlinia's press, his business seems to have been taken on by Richard Pynson, whose first dated book appeared in 1493. Though it is impossible to prove conclusively that Pynson succeeded Machlinia in business, many small points seem to show that this was the case. We find leaves of Machlinia's books in bindings undoubtedly produced by Pynson, and he was also in possession of a border used by Machlinia in his edition of the *Sarum Horæ*. It is often said that Pynson was an apprentice of Caxton's ; but we have no evidence of this beyond the words in the prologue to the *Chaucer*, where Caxton is called 'my worshipful master'—a title applied sometimes to Caxton by printers living fifty years after.[1]

In his patent of naturalisation of 30th July 1513, Pynson is described as a native of Normandy ; and we know that he had business relations with Le Talleur of Rouen, who printed some law-books for him. These books, three in number, may be ascribed to about 1490, or to some time after Machlinia had ceased printing, and before Pynson had begun It was probably very soon after 1490 that Pynson set up his printing establishment at the Temple Bar ; for though his first dated book, the *Dives and Pauper*, is dated the 5th July 1493, there are one or two other books that can with certainty be placed before it.

A fragment of a grammar, consisting of the last leaf only, among the Hearne fragments in the Bodleian, is all that remains of one of his earliest books. It is printed entirely in his first large coarse type, which bears so much resemblance to some of Machlinia's ; and was used as waste to line the boards of a book before Passion Week, 1494.

The *Chaucer*, in which two types are used, one for the prose and another for the verse, is also earlier

---

[1] Blades, in his *Life of Caxton*, not only says that Pynson was Caxton's apprentice, but that he used his mark in some of his books. This mistake has arisen from a doctored copy of Bonaventure's *Speculum vite Christi* in the British Museum, which has a leaf with Caxton's device inserted at the end.

IN Beneracione nois dilectissimi filii tui
dñi nri iħu cristi tibi deus pater miarū de
uotis mētibz hostias immolamus/ suppliciter
depcantes/ Vt earū virtute cunctis egentibus/
prestetur auxiliū ҁ in eodē noīe delectantes sa
lutarē sui propositi consequantur effectū. Per
eundē. Prefacio/   Quia p īcarnati.   Coīm.
Vincenti dado manna absconditum ҁ dado il
ci calculū candidum et in calculo nomen nouū
scriptū quob nemo sit nisi qui accipit.

SAcro sancta misteria ҁ sūp   ⸿Postcoīm
simus domine ad honorē nois cōplacen
tissimi fili tui dñi nri iħu cristi deuotis pcordiis
recolentes/ quesumus vt lcremēta spūalis ex
ultacionis accumulent ҁ effectum nostrum ad
hoc salutiferū nomen nobis iugit lprimenduz
accendant ҁ ad iubilacionē; iubilandū in iħesu
saluatori nro dulcissimo tota mentis intencōe
promoueant. Per eundem dominū nrm iħm.
Per totas oct dicat missa predict qñ de octauis
agitur seb sine Credo.   Sequencia per octa.
Jesus pulcer in decore. ҁc.

Per me Ricardum Pinson.

FROM THE 'FESTUM NOMINIS JESU.'
PYNSON, C. 1493.

than the *Dives and Pauper*. It is illustrated with a number of badly executed woodcuts, cut specially for the book, of the various pilgrims in the *Canterbury Tales*. Some of these cuts were altered while the book was passing through the press, and serve again for different characters. The Sergeaunt with a little alteration reappears as the Doctor of Physick, and the Squire is turned into the Manciple.

In 1493 the *Dives and Pauper* appeared. It is printed in a new type, copied evidently from a French model, and strongly resembling some used in Verard's books. This type superseded the larger type of the *Chaucer*, which we do not find in use again. To 1493 a number of small books can be assigned, all printed in the type of the *Dives and Pauper*, and having twenty-five lines to the page. Amongst them we may mention the *Festum Nominis Jesu;* an edition of Lydgate's *Churl and Bird;* a *Life of St. Margaret*, which is known only from fragments, and a legal work of which there is one leaf in Lambeth Palace Library.

The method of using signatures, which Pynson adopted in these early books, affords another small piece of evidence to prove that he learnt to print at Rouen, and not in England. In the quartos, the first leaf of the quire is signed A 1, the second has no signature, while the third is signed A 2. This way of signing (by the sheet instead of by the leaf), not a very ordinary one, was commonly in use at Rouen ; while Caxton and De Worde signed in the more usual manner, with consecutive signatures to each leaf for the first half of the quire.

For some unknown reason, Pynson was dissatisfied with the *Dives and Pauper* type, for after 1493 it never seems to have been used again. From this time onwards, till about 1500, the majority of his books were printed in the small type of the *Chaucer*, or in some newer types of a more severe and less French appearance. In his earliest books Pynson used a device consisting of his initials cut in wood, so as to print white upon a black background. It resembles in many ways that of his old associate Le Talleur, and may therefore have been cut in Rouen. In 1496 we find him using two new devices, one a large woodcut containing his mark, and a helmet surmounted by a small bird,[1] which began to break about 1497, and was soon disused. The other, which is a metal cut, is in two pieces, a border of men and flowers, and an interior piece with the mark on a shield and supporters. The border of this device is a most useful guide in determining the dates of the books in which it occurs. In the lower part is a ribbon pierced for the insertion of type. The two ends of the piece below the ribbon were too thin to be strong, so that the piece gets gradually bent in, the ribbon becoming narrower and narrower. According to the bend of this piece the exact year can be

---

[1] The bird above the helmet is a finch, no doubt a punning allusion to Pynson's name, Pynson being the Norman word for a finch. Very probably the birds in the large coat of arms are finches also, though Ames calls them eagles.

ascertained, from 1499, when it began to get displaced, to 1513, when it broke off altogether.

Among the books which appeared in 1494, the *Fall of Princis*, translated by Lydgate from Boccaccio, is the most remarkable. It is printed throughout in the smaller type of the *Chaucer*, and at the head of each part is a woodcut of particularly good execution. The copy of this book in the British Museum, unfortunately imperfect, was rescued from the counter of a small shop where it was being used to make little bags or 'twists' to hold pennyworths of sweets. Each leaf has been divided into four pieces. A *Grammar of Sulpitius* and a *Book of Good Manners* were also printed with a date in this year. In 1495 no dated books were issued, but the *Petronylla* and *The Art and Craft to know well to Dye* must have been issued about this time. In 1496, Pynson printed a small supplement to the first edition of the *Hymns and Sequences* printed at Cologne by Quentell, and in the following year he issued a complete edition of the book, and an edition of the *Horæ ad usum Sarum*. In the same year (1497) he printed six of Terence's plays, each signed separately so that they could be issued apart. About this year were issued two interesting folios, *Reynard the Fox*, and a *Speculum vite Christi*, with illustrations. In 1500 was issued the *Book of Cookery*, of which the only known copy is in the library at Longleat, and the splendid *Sarum Missal*, printed at the expense of Cardinal Morton, and generally known as the Morton Missal. Of undated books printed about this time we may notice especially, editions of *Guy of Warwick, Maundeville's Travels, Informatio Puerorum,* a few small school-books, and a number of year-books and other legal works.

About 1502–3, Pynson changed his residence from outside Temple Bar to the George in Fleet Street, where he continued to the end of his life. His career as a printer is curiously different from Wynkyn de Worde's. The latter was the popular printer, publishing numbers of slight books of a kind likely to appeal to the public. Pynson, on the other hand, was in a more official position as King's printer, and seems to have been generally chosen as the publisher of learned books. Wynkyn de Worde printed ten slight books for every one of a more solid character; with Pynson the average was about equal.

From 1510 onwards we find frequent entries relating to Pynson in all the accounts of payments made by Henry VIII., and these show that he was clearly the royal printer, and in receipt of an annuity. In September 1509, he issued the *Sermo fratris Hieronymi de Ferraria,* which contains the first Roman type used in England. In 1513 appeared the *Sege and Dystruccyon of Troye,* of which there are several copies known, printed upon vellum.

Pynson's will is dated 18th November 1529, and was proved on 18th February 1530. He was succeeded in business by Robert Redman, who had been for a few years previously his rather unscrupulous rival.

The last few years of the fifteenth century saw a great change in the development of English printing. Up to the time of Caxton's death in 1491, there seems to have been little foreign competition, but immediately after this date the state of things altered entirely. Both France and Italy produced books for the English market, and sent over stationers to dispose of them. Gerard Leeu at Antwerp printed a number of English books, mostly of a popular character, while Hertzog in Venice, and a number of printers in Paris, printed service-books of Sarum use.

By 1493 two stationers were settled in England ; one, Frederick Egmondt, as an agent for Hertzog, the other, Nicholas Lecompte, who sold books printed in Paris. Though we only know of these two as stationers through their names appearing in the colophons of books with which they were connected, there must have been many others of whom we have no trace. After the Act of 1483, which so strongly encouraged foreign importations, a very large number of books for the English market were printed abroad. This was at first occasioned by the small variety in the number of types and the scarcity of ornamental letters and woodcuts. In 1487, Caxton commissioned George Maynyal, a Paris printer, to print an edition of the *Sarum Missal*, and this is the first foreign printed book for sale in England whose history we know. About ten years previously, a *Sarum Breviary* had been printed at Cologne, and in 1483 another edition at Venice. The first edition of the *Sarum*

Missal was printed about 1486 by Wenssler at Basle. In the fifteenth century, at least fifty books are known to have been printed abroad for sale in England. Most of these were service-books, but there were a few of other classes. Gerard Leeu reprinted three of Caxton's books, *The Chronicles*, *The History of Jason*, and the *History of Paris and the fair Vienne*, and added a fourth popular book to these, which had not previously appeared in English, the *Dialogues of Salomon and Marcolphus*. In addition to these, he printed editions of the *Sarum Directorium Sacerdotum* and *Horæ*.

Another class of books produced abroad were school-books, and the earliest of these for English use is an edition of the grammatical tracts of *Perottus*, printed at Louvain in 1486 by Egidius van der Heerstraten. In the same year Leeu printed the *Vulgaria*, and very shortly afterwards editions of the Grammars by Anwykyll and the *Garlandia* were issued from Deventer, Antwerp, Cologne, and Paris.

The greater portion, however, of this foreign importation consisted of service-books, at least forty editions being sent over from abroad before 1501. From Venice were sent Breviaries and Missals, printed for the most part by Johannes de Landoia dictus Hertog. As we have said, the first edition of the *Sarum Breviary* was printed at Cologne by an unknown printer, and the first edition of the *Sarum Missal* at Basle by Wenssler about 1486. From Paris and Rouen came the greater number of *Horæ*, and such books as the *Legenda, Manuale,* and *Liber Festivalis.*

It is impossible to enter here with any fulness into the history of the earliest stationers and the books printed abroad for sale in England. It is rather foreign to our present subject, but would well repay careful study.

CHAPTER XI.

THE introduction of printing into Scotland did not take place till 1508, in which year a printer named Andrew Myllar set up his press in the Southgait at Edinburgh. At this time the countries of Scotland and France were in close business communications, and many Scotsmen sought employment on the Continent. In 1496 a certain David Lauxius, a native of Edinburgh, was in the employment of Hopyl, the Paris printer, as a press corrector, an employment often undertaken by men of learning. Lauxius afterwards became a schoolmaster at Arras, and is several times spoken of by Badius Ascensius in the prefatory letters which he prefixed to his grammars. Such books as were needed were sent over to Scotland from France, and the probable cause of the introduction of printing into the former country was the desire of William Elphinstone, Bishop of Aberdeen, to have his adaptation of the *Sarum Breviary* for the use of Aberdeen produced under his own personal supervision. Two men were readily found to undertake the work; one, Walter Chepman, a wealthy merchant, who supplied the necessary capital; the other, Andrew Myllar, a bookseller, who had several times employed foreign presses to print books for him, and had himself been abroad on business expeditions.

The books which had been printed for Myllar were, *Multorum vocabulorum equivocorum interpretatio magistri Johannis de Garlandia*, in 1505, and *Expositio sequentiarum secundum usum Sarum*, in 1506; both being without a printer's name, but most probably from the press of P. Violette of Rouen.[1]

As was to be expected, Myllar obtained his type from France, and probably from Rouen, but it bears no resemblance to that used in the books printed for him. Among the Rouen types it is most like that used by Le Talleur, but the resemblance is not very close. The capital letters seem identical with those used by De Marnef, at Paris, in his *Nef des folz*, and are also very like those of the Lyons printer, Claude Daygne.

Supplied with these types, Myllar returned to Edinburgh, and in the spring of 1508 issued a series of nine poetical pamphlets, the only known copies being now preserved in the Advocates' Library, Edinburgh. These were all issued within a few days of

[1] Dr. Dickson, relying on the authority of M. Claudin, has ascribed these books to the press of Lawrence Hostingue of Rouen. From the facsimiles which he gives it is clear that the types are not identical. The books should rather be ascribed to Pierre Violette, who used, as far as can be seen, the same type; and who also used in his *Expositio Hymnorum et Sequentiarum ad usum Sarum*, printed in 1507, the woodcut of a man seated at a reading desk, which is found on the title-page of Myllar's *Garlandia*.

each other, and neither the type nor the woodcuts show any indication of wear or blemishes which might enable some order to be assigned to them. These books, like Pynson's early quartos, are signed by the sheet, an indication that the printer learnt his art at Rouen.

In 1510 the *Breviary* was issued, and, were it not for the colophon, would pass as the production of a Norman press. It is in two volumes; the Pars Hiemalis, containing 400 leaves, the Pars Estivalis, 378. Only four copies are known, all imperfect. With the production of this book the Edinburgh press stopped for some while.

There is no doubt much yet to be learnt about the history of the first Scottish press, especially in its relations to those of Normandy, and there seems no reason why in time it should not become quite clear. Not only are the original books in existence, but also the acts relating to them. One other book must be noticed as having been printed in Scotland before 1530. This is the *De compassione Beate Virginis Marie*, a 'novum festum' issued for incorporation into the *Breviary*, and printed at Edinburgh, by John Story, about 1520. Of this little tract but one copy remains, which is bound up in the copy of the *Aberdeen Breviary* belonging to Lord Strathmore at Glamis. It consists of a single sheet of eight leaves, and, according to Dr. Dickson, is not printed in the same type as the *Breviary*.

From this time onward till Davidson began to

print, it seems as though Scotland had no practised typographer. Hector Boece, John Vaus, and others, were obliged to send their books to be printed at a foreign press; Vaus indeed went over to Paris to superintend the printing of his Grammar by Badius, who was at that time the printer most favoured by Scottish authors.

No book was actually printed at York till 1509, but for many years before that date there had been stationers in the city who imported foreign books for sale. Frederick Frees, who was enrolled as a freeman in 1497, is spoken of as a book printer, but no specimen of his work exists. His brother Gerard, who assumed the surname of Wanseford, imported in 1507 an edition of the *Sarum Hymns and Sequences*, printed for him at Rouen by P. Violette. Of this book only two copies are known. Shortly after Gerard Wanseford's death, an action was brought against his executor, Ralph Pulleyn, by Frederick Frees, the brother, about the stock of books which had been left, and which consisted mostly of servicebooks, bound and unbound, with some *alphabeta* and others in Latin and English.

In 1509 a certain Hugo Goes printed an edition of the *Directorium Sacerdotum*, the first dated book printed at York. Two copies are known, one in the Chapter Library at York, and the other in the library of Sidney Sussex College, Cambridge. Davies [1]

[1] Davies' *Memoir of the York Press*, 1868, 8vo, pp. 16–18.

M

incorrectly states that both copies are imperfect, and want the leaf upon which the colophon was printed; but it is certainly in the Cambridge copy, for this wants only the last leaf, which would either be blank or with a printer's mark. The book is for the most part printed in the type which W. de Worde used at Westminster just before 1500. Goes printed also editions of the *Donatus* and *Accidence*, but no copies are now known, though in 1667 copies were in possession of a Mr. Hildyard, a York historian. Bagford, among his notes on printing [Harl. MS. 5974, 95], mentions a *Donatus cum Remigio*, 'impressus Londiniis juxta Charing Cross per me Hugonem Goes and Henery Watson'—with the printer's device H. G. This book also is unknown, but may perhaps be the Grammar mentioned by Ames as being among Lord Oxford's books. If the copy of the colophon is correct, it shows that Goes was at some time printing in London. He is said to have also printed at Beverley.

In 1516, 'Ursyn Milner, prynter,' was admitted to the freedom of the city. He was born in 1481, and by 1511 was living in York, when he gave evidence in the suit between Ralph Pulleyn and Frederick Frees. He printed only two books, a *Festum visitationis Beate Marie Virginis*, and a *Grammar* of Whittington's.

The *Festum* was issued doubtless between 1513 and 1515, for in 1513 the Convocation of York ordered the feast of the Visitation of the Blessed Virgin Mary to be kept as a 'Festum principale.' It is quoted

by Ames, p. 468, and has the following colophon :
'Feliciter finiunt (?) festum visitationis beate Marie
virginis secundum usum ebor. Noviter impressum
per Ursyn Milner commorantem in cimiterio Minsterii
Sancti Petri.' It is in 8vo, and a copy formerly
belonged to Thomas Rawlinson.

The second book, the *Grammar*, is a quarto of
twenty-four leaves, made up in quires of eight and
four leaves alternately, a peculiar system of quiring
much affected by Wynkyn de Worde. Below the
title is a cut of a schoolmaster with three pupils,
which was used by Wynkyn de Worde in 1499, and
which he in turn had obtained from Govaert van
Ghemen about 1490. (The cut was first used in the
Opusculum Grammaticale, Gouda, 13th November
1486.) Below the colophon, which tells us that the
book was printed in 'blake-strete' on the 20th
December 1516, is the printer's device, consisting of
a shield hanging on a tree supported by a bear and
an ass, the bear being an allusion to his name Ursyn.
On the shield are a sun and a windmill, the latter
referring to his surname Milner. Below this device
is an oblong cut containing his name in full on a
ribbon, his trade-mark being in the centre.

The connexion between the early York stationers
and Wynkyn de Worde is very striking, and has yet
to be explained. Gerard Wanseford in his will, dated
1510, leaves forty shillings to Wynkyn de Worde,
which he (the testator) owed him. The next stationer
and printer, Hugo Goes, was in possession of some

of De Worde's type; and Milner, the last of the early
York printers, used one of his cuts, and copies his
peculiar habit of quiring. Perhaps the type and cuts
were originally bought by Wanseford and obtained
successively by the others ; at any rate, both the type
and cut were out of W. de Worde's hands at an early
date.

The most important of the York stationers
remains still to be noticed, though he was unfortunately only a stationer and not a printer. John
Gachet appears at York in 1517, and in the same
year is mentioned as a stationer at Hereford. He
was in business in the former town at least as late
as 1533, when the last book printed at his expense
was issued.

Printing was introduced into Cambridge in 1521,
when John Lair de Siberch, perhaps at the instigation
of Richard Croke, who from 1522 was professor of
Greek and public orator, set up his press at the sign
of the Arma Regia. In 1521 he printed six books,
and of these the *Oratio Henrici Bulloci* is the first.
The five other books follow in the following order :
Augustini Sermo, Luciani περὶ διψάδων, *Balduini
sermo de altaris sacramento, Erasmus de conscribendis
epistolis*, and *Galeni de Temperamentis*. In the
next year Siberch printed only two books, *Joannis
Roffensis episcopi contio*, and *Papyrii Gemini Eleatis
Hermathena*. It is needless to describe these books
more fully here, for an extremely good and full

bibliography of them was compiled by Bradshaw, and published as an introduction to one of the Cambridge facsimiles in 1886.[1]

Since the publication of this bibliography, the existence of another book from the first Cambridge press has been discovered. In 1889, among some other fragments forming the covers of a book in Westminster Abbey Library, were found part of the first sheet of the Cambridge *Papyrius Geminus*, and two leaves of a grammar in the same type, in quarto, with twenty-six lines to the page besides headlines. These turned out to be part of the small grammar, *De octo orationis partium constructione*, written for use in Paul's School. It was written by Lily and amended by Erasmus, and finally issued anonymously. After the printing of these nine books Siberch is lost sight of; but that he was still alive in 1525 we know from a letter of Erasmus, who, writing on Christmas Day to Dr. Robert Aldrich of King's College, sends greetings, among others, to 'Gerardum, Nicolaum et Joannem Siburgum bibliopolas.' Amongst the fragments taken from the binding spoken of above, was a letter to Siberch from the well-known Antwerp and London bookseller, Peter Kaetz, relating to the purchase of books, but it has unfortunately no date, though certainly earlier than 1524.

---

[1] *Doctissimi viri Henrici Bulloci Oratio . . .* reproduced in facsimile . . . with a bibliographical introduction by the late Henry Bradshaw, M.A. Cambridge, 1886. 4to.

Two books were printed at Tavistock in the first half of the sixteenth century; and as the monks possessed a printing press of their own, it is quite probable that other books were issued which have now entirely perished. The first book is an English metrical translation of the *De Consolatione Philosophiæ* of Boethius made by Thomas Waltwnem. It has the following colophon: 'Emprented in the exempt monastery of Tavestock in Denshyre. By me Dan Thomas Rychard, monke of the sayd monastery. To the instant desyre of the ryght worshypful esquyer Mayster Robert Langdon, anno d. MDXXV.' Several copies of this book are known.

Of the other book but one copy is known, now in the library of Exeter College, Oxford. It is a small quarto of twenty-six leaves, with thirty or thirty-one lines to the page. The title runs, 'Here foloyth the confirmation of the Charter perteynynge to all the tynners wythyn the countey of Devonshyre, wyth there statutes also made at Crockeryntorre by the hole assent and consent of al the sayd tynners yn the yere of the reygne of our souerayne Lord Kynge Henry ye VIII. the secund yere.' The book ends on the reverse of signature d 3, 'Here endyth the statutes of the stannary. Imprented yn Tavystoke ye xx day of August the yere of the reygne off our soveryne Lord Kynge Henry ye VIII. the xxvi yere.'

At Abingdon a book was printed in 1528 by John Scolar, who had been printing at Oxford about ten years previously. It is the *Breviary* for the use of Abingdon, and the only known copy is in the library of Emmanuel College, Cambridge. The colophon runs : 'Istud portiforium fuit impressum per Joannem Scholarem in monasterio beate marie virginis Abendonensi. Anno incarnationis dominice Millesimo quingentesimo vicesimo octavo. Et Thome Rowlonde abbatis septimo decimo.'

Two other towns must be mentioned, which, though not possessing resident printers, had stationers who published books printed for them. In 1505 the Hereford *Breviary* was issued under the superintendence of Inghelbert Haghe, and under the patronage of the 'Illustrissime viraginis,' Margaret, Countess of Richmond and Derby. It has the following colophon : 'Impressum est hoc breviarium secundum eiusdem diocesis usum in clarissimo rathomagensi emporio: impensis et cura Inghelberti Haghe dicte comitis bibliopole ac dedititii. Anno salutis christi Millesimo quingentesimo quinto. 11. non. augusti.' Of this book only three copies are known. One, textually perfect, and containing both parts, is in Worcester Cathedral Library. The Bodleian has a Pars Estivalis, slightly imperfect, and another copy is in private hands. We can trace this bookseller to a later date, for his name occurs in a note written on a fragment in the Bodleian, which formed at one time the lining of a binding, 'Dedi bibliopole herfordensi Ingleberto nuncupato pro isto et sex reliquis libris biblie xliii^s iiij^d quos emi ludlowie anno domini incarnationis millesimo quingentesimo decimo circiter die nundinarum lichefeldensium.'

The other town is Exeter, where, about 1510, a stationer named Martin Coeffin was living. Two books were printed for him, both of which were without date. One of these was the *Vocabula magistri Stanbrigi, primum jam edita, sua saltem editione,* printed, so Ames tells us, by Lawrence Hostingue and Jamet Loys at Rouen. He adds further, that the 'piece' had five leaves, which we may take to be impossible; it must have had six leaves, of which the last was blank, or had a printer's device upon it. The second book was a *Catho cum commento,* printed at Rouen by Richard Goupil, 'juxta conventum sancti Augustini ad intersignum regulæ auræ commorantis.' On the subject of this book Ames is no more explicit; he tells us it was printed at the expense of Martin Coeffin at Exeter, beyond that he has nothing to say. The two pieces are quoted by him in his *General History of Printing* between the years 1510 and 1517, and the date which he thus assigns is probably fairly correct, for Frère quotes Goupil under the year 1510, and Hostingue under 1505–10.

CHAPTER XII.

THE STUDY OF BOOKBINDING.

TOO little attention has been paid, in this country at any rate, to the fact that some knowledge about early bookbinding is essential to the student of early printing. At first the printer was also a stationer and bookbinder, and the three occupations were hardly clearly defined or definitely separated within the first hundred years after the invention of printing. Books always required some kind of binding, and the early printer sold his books to the purchaser ready bound, though copies seem always to have been obtainable in sheets by such as wished them in that state. The binder ornamented his books in certain ways and with a limited number of stamps, and there is no reason why a careful study should not make his binding ornamentation as easily recognisable as his woodcuts or his type. Of course the majority of early bindings are unsigned, and therefore it is not often possible to assign particular bindings to particular men ; but comparison may enable us to attribute them to particular districts and even to particular places, so that they may often afford additional evidence towards placing books which contain no information of their origin.

A very little attention paid to a binding might often result in most valuable information, and with the destruction of the binding the information disappears. Many years ago there came into the hands of a certain Mr. Horn a very valuable volume consisting of three block-books, the *Biblia Pauperum*, the *Ars Moriendi*, and the *Apocalypse*, all bound together, and in their original binding, which was dated. Incredible as it may seem, the volume was split up and the binding destroyed. Mr. Horn asserted from memory that the date was 1428; of the first three figures he was sure, and of the last he was more or less certain. Naturally the date has been questioned, and it has been surmised that the 2 must have been some other figure which Mr. Horn deciphered incorrectly. The destruction of the binding made it impossible that this question could ever be set at rest, and a very important date in the history of printing was lost absolutely.

In the last century no regard whatever seems to have been paid to old bindings, the very fact of their being old prejudiced librarians against them; if they became damaged or worn they were not repaired, but destroyed, and the book rebound. Nor did they fare better in earlier times. Somewhere in the first half of the seventeenth century all the manuscripts in the Cambridge University Library were uniformly rebound in rough calf, to the utter destruction of every trace of their former history.

Casley, in his catalogue of the manuscripts in the

Royal Library, specially mentions a curious old binding, with an inscription showing that it was made at Oxford, in Catte Street, in 1467. Even the special note in the catalogue did not save this binding, which, if it had been preserved, would have been one of the earliest, if not the earliest, dated English example.

There is no need to multiply examples to show how widespread the destruction of old bindings has been as regards public libraries; indeed, their escaping without observation was their only chance of escaping without destruction. In private libraries much the same thing has happened. The great collectors of the period of Dibdin thought nothing worthy of notice unless 'encased' in a russia or morocco leather covering by Lewis or some bookbinder of the time. Nor are collectors of the same opinion now obsolete, for many of our better known binders can show specimens of rare and interesting old bindings which they have been ordered to strip off and replace with something new. Ignorance is the cause of much of what we lament. So many collectors are ruled entirely by the advice of their booksellers and binders, and these in their turn are influenced purely by commercial instincts. Collectors with knowledge or opinions of their own are beginning to see that the one thing which makes a book valuable (not simply in the way of pounds, shillings, and pence) is that it shall be, as far as possible, in its original condition. Our greatest

books of the seventeenth century were issued in
simple calf bindings, with no attempt at ornamentation
but a plain line ruled down the cover about an inch
from the back. If a collector wants modern
ornamental bindings, let him put them on modern
books, there only are they not out of place.

About the German binders, who necessarily con-
cern us most at the time of the invention of printing,
we know very little; but, on the other hand, there is
a great deal to be learnt. Their bindings, both of
pigskin and calf, are impressed with a large number
of very beautiful and carefully executed dies, which
could with a little care be separated into groups.
Many of them, curiously enough, are very similar to
some used on London and Durham bindings of the
twelfth and thirteenth centuries. There are the same
palm-leaf dies and drop-shaped stamps containing
dragons.

It is in Germany that the earliest dated bindings
are found. A copy of the Eggesteyn forty-one line
Bible, in the Cambridge University Library, has the
date 1464 impressed on the metal bosses which pro-
tect the corners ; and as the book is without a colophon, this date is of importance. A binder named
Jean Richenbach dated all his bindings, and added,
as a rule, the name of the person for whom they were
bound. The earliest date we have for him is 1467,
and they run from that year to 1475. Johannes
Fogel is another name often found on early German
bindings. A few printers' names occur, such as

Ambrose Keller, Veldener, Zainer, Amorbach. About the time of Koburger, great changes were introduced into the style of German binding, a harmonious design being produced by means of large tools, and the use of small dies given up. The custom was also introduced of printing the title on the side in gold. The panel stamp, so popular in other countries, was not much used in Germany for calf books; it is found, however, on innumerable pigskin and parchment bindings of the latter half of the sixteenth century. The earliest of the bindings of this class have often the boards of wood; at a later date they are almost invariably of paper or millboard. On early French books the work is finer, but as a rule less interesting; but the panel stamps, especially the early ones, are very good. A very large number are signed in full. One with the name of Alexandre Alyat, a Paris stationer, is particularly fine, as are also the series belonging to Jean Norins. The Norman binders produced work very like the English, no doubt because many of the books printed there were intended especially for the English market.

The bookbinding of the Low Countries was always fine; but the great improvement which was first introduced there was the use of the panel stamp, invented about the middle of the fourteenth century. It was not till after the introduction of printing, and when books were issued of a small size, that this invention became of real importance; but at the

end of the fifteenth and during the first twenty or
thirty years of the sixteenth centuries, innumerable
bindings of this class were produced. The majority
of Netherlandish panels are not pictorial, but are
ornamented with a double row of fabulous beasts
and birds in circles of foliage; round this runs a
legend, very often containing the binder's name.
*Discere ne cesses cura sapientia crescit Martinus
Vulcanius* is on one binding; on another, *Ob laudem
christi hunc librum recte ligavi Johannes Bollcaert.*
Some binders give not only their name, but the
place also—*Johannes de Wowdix Antwerpie me fecit.*
Though there are few pictorial Flemish panels, some
of these are not without interest. A number were
produced by a binder whose initials are I. P., and
who was connected in some way with the Augustinian Monastery of St. Gregory and St. Martin at
Louvain. One which contains a medallion head, a
small figure of Cleopatra, and a good deal of arab-
esque ornament of foliage, is his best; while another
panel, large enough for a quarto book, with a border
of chain work, and his initials on a shield in the
centre, is his rarest, and is in its way very artistic.
At a still later date the binders in the Low Countries
produced some panels, which, though still pictorial,
show how rapidly the art was being debased. The
designs are ill drawn, and the inscription, originally an important part, has come to be degraded
into a piece of ornamentation without meaning, cut
by the engraver purely with that object, ignoring the

individual letters or legibility of the inscription, and anxious only that the finish which an inscription gave to his models might be apparent to the eye in his copies. A similar debasement is not uncommon in late English examples.

Italian and Spanish binding, though interesting in itself, affords little information as regards printers or stationers. No bindings were signed, and the designs are in all cases so similar as to afford little clue to the place from which they originally came.

The earliest English bindings are extremely interesting and distinctive. Caxton, our first printer, always bound his books in leather, never making use of vellum or pigskin. Bindings of wrapping vellum, which he is erroneously said to have made, were not used in England till a very much later period. His bindings, if ornamented at all, were ruled with diagonal lines, and in the centre of each compartment thus formed a die was impressed. A border was often placed round the side, formed from triangular stamps pointing alternately inwards and outwards, these stamps containing the figure of a dragon.

The number of bindings which can with certainty be ascribed to Caxton is necessarily small. We can, in the first place, only take those on books printed by him, and which contain, besides this, distinct evidence, from the end-papers or fragments used in the binding, that they came from his workshop. Under this class we can place the cover of the *Boethius*, discovered in the Grammar School at St. Alban's, an edition of the *Festial* in the British Museum, and a few others; and from the stamps used on these we can identify others which have no other indication. It must always be remembered that these dies were almost indestructible, and therefore were often in use long after their original owner was dead. The Oxford bindings, though very English in design, are stamped with dies Netherlandish in origin. An ornament of three small circles arranged in a triangle occurs very often on these bindings, and is a very distinctive one. These bindings when in their original condition are almost always, like those of the Netherlands, lined with vellum, and have vellum guards to the centre of the quires. The only two copies known of one of Caxton's indulgences were found pasted face downwards, used to line the binding of a Netherland printed book. Another binder, about the end of the fifteenth century, whose initials, G. W., and mark occur on a shield-shaped die, used always printed matter to line his bindings and make end-papers, though they were not necessarily on vellum. All the leaves now known of the Machlinia *Horæ ad usum Sarum* whose provenance can be ascertained, came from bindings by this man, scattered about in different parts of the country. It is not known in what part of the country he worked.

Trade bindings between 1500 and 1540 form an

James Hyatt.

PYNSON BINDING.

important series. All small books were stamped with a panel on the sides, and these often have the initials or mark of the binder. Pynson used a stamp with his device upon it; many others used two panels, with the arms of England on one side and the Tudor rose on the other, both with supporters. On the majority of these panels, below the rose, is the binder's mark and initials; on the other side, below the shield, his initials alone. Not many of these binders' or stationers' names have been discovered, and there are few materials to enable us to do so. Pynson and Julian Notary's bindings have the same devices as they used in their books, and some of Jacobi's have the mark which occurs on the title-page to the *Lyndewode* of 1506 printed for him. Reynes' various marks are well known and of common occurrence.

Without a distinguishing mark of some kind beyond the initials, it is hopeless to try and ascribe bindings to particular stationers, though a careful examination of the style or evidences as to early ownership may help us to determine with some accuracy the country at least from which the binding comes. Even a study of the forwarding of a binding is of great help. The method of sewing and putting on headbands is quite different in Italian books from those of other countries. Again, all small books were, as a rule, sewn on three bands in England and Normandy; in other countries the rule is for them to have four. The leather gives sometimes a clue, *e.g.* in parts of France sheepskin

was used in place of calf. Cambridge bindings can
often be recognised from a peculiar red colouring of
the leather. So little has been done as yet to classify
the different peculiarities of style or work in these
early bindings, that it can hardly be expected that
much should be known about them ; at present the
study is still in its infancy, but there is no doubt that,
if persevered in, it will have valuable results. These
bindings were for the most part produced, certainly in
the sixteenth century, by men who were not printers,
and whose names we have consequently few chances
of discovering. All that can therefore be done is to
classify them according to style, and according to
such extraneous information as may be available. It
is useless with no other information to attempt to
assign initials.

But while the bindings and the designs afford
valuable information, the materials employed in
making the bindings are also of great importance.
The boards were often made of refuse printed leaves
pasted together, and were always lined, after the
binding was completed, with leaves of paper or vellum,
printed or manuscript. On this subject I cannot do
better than give the following quotation from one of
Henry Bradshaw's Memoranda, No. 5, *Notice of the
Bristol fragment of the Fifteen Oes* :—

'After all that has been said, it cannot be any
matter of wonder that the fragments used for lining
the boards of old books should have an interest for
those who make a study of the methods and habits of

our early printers, with a view to the solution of some
of many difficulties still remaining unsettled in the
history of printing. I have for many years tried to
draw the attention of librarians and others to the
evidence which may be gleaned from a careful study
from these fragments, and if done systematically and
intelligently, it ceases to be mere antiquarian potter-
ing or aimless waste of time. I have elsewhere drawn
attention [1] to the distinction to be observed between
what may be called respectively *binder's waste* and
printer's waste. When speaking of fragments of
books as *binder's waste*, I mean books which have
been in circulation, and have been thrown away as
useless. The value of such fragments is principally in
themselves. They may or may not be of interest.
But by *printer's waste* I mean . . . waste, proof, or
cancelled sheets in the printer's office, which, in the
early days when printers were their own bookbinders,
would be used by the bookbinder for lining the
boards, or the centres of quires, of books bound in the
same office where they were printed. In this way
such fragments have a value beyond themselves, as
they enable us to infer almost with certainty that
such books are specimens of the binding executed in
the office of the printer who printed them ; and thus,
once seeing the style adopted and the actual designs
used, we are able to recognise the same binder's work,

---

[1] Lists of Founts of Type and Woodcut Devices used by printers in
Holland in the Fifteenth Century. Memorandum No. 3. No. 14 in
the *Collected Papers*.

even when there are none of these waste sheets to lead us to the same conclusion.'

The number of books known only from fragments rescued from bindings is much larger than is generally supposed. Of books printed in England before 1530 more than ten per cent. are only known in this way; and now that more attention is being paid to the subject, remains of unknown books are continually being discovered.

Blades in his *Life of Caxton* [edit. 1861, vol. ii. p. 70] gives a most interesting account of a find of this sort in the library of the St. Alban's Grammar School. 'After examining a few interesting books, I pulled out one which was lying flat upon the top of others. It was in a most deplorable state, covered thickly with a damp, sticky dust, and with a considerable portion of the back rotted away by wet. The white decay fell in lumps on the floor as the unappreciated volume was opened. It proved to be Geoffrey Chaucer's English translation of *Boecius de consolatione Philosophiæ*, printed by Caxton, in the original binding as issued from Caxton's workshop, and uncut! . . . On dissecting the covers they were found to be composed entirely of waste sheets from Caxton's press, two or three being printed on one side only. The two covers yielded no less than fifty-six half-sheets of printed paper, proving the existence of three works from Caxton's press quite unknown before.'

Off a stall in Booksellers Row the writer some few years ago bought for a couple of shillings an imperfect foreign printed folio of about 1510 in an original stamped binding, lined at each end with printed leaves. From one end came the title-page and another leaf of an unknown English *Donatus* printed by Guillam Faques ; from the other end, two leaves, one having the mark and colophon of a hitherto unknown book printed by Richard Faques, and which is at present the earliest book known to have been issued from his press. The finding of these two fragments is further of interest as showing a connection between the two printers called Faques.

Nor do these early fragments always come out of very old bindings. From a sixpenny box at Salisbury the writer bought a large folio of divinity, printed about 1700, in its original plain calf binding. The end leaves were complete pages of the first book printed in London, the *Questiones Antonii Andreæ*, printed by Lettou in 1480.

The boards of a book in Westminster Abbey Library, which must have been bound at Cambridge in the second quarter of the sixteenth century, were composed of leaves of the *Pontanus de Roma*, one of the ' Costeriana.'

Service-books were very largely used by the bookbinders, for the many Acts passed for their mutilation or destruction soon turned the majority of copies into waste paper. Several copies of Henry VIII.'s *Letters to Martin Luther* of 1526, which remain in their original bindings, have their boards made of such material, a practical commentary on the King's opinions.

Manuscripts, many of the utmost importance, have been cut up by the bookbinders; sometimes in early days the librarian handed out what he considered a useless manuscript to the bookbinder whom he employed. Bradshaw notes that Edward VI.'s own copy of the Stephen's *Greek Testament* of 1550 contains in the binding large fragments of an early manuscript of Horace and Persius. Vellum was often used in early books to line the centre of each quire so as to prevent the paper being cut by the thread used for the sewing. Many pieces of *Donatuses* and *Indulgences* have been found in this manner cut up into long strips about half an inch wide. The copy of the Gotz *Bible* of 1480 in Jesus College, Cambridge, bound in London by Lettou, has the centres of the quires lined with strips of two editions of an indulgence printed by him, and which are otherwise unknown.

When the leaves used to line the boards of an old book are valuable or important, they should be carefully taken out, if this can be done without injury to the binding or to the fragments. A note should at once be put on the fragments stating from what book they were taken, and a note should also be put in the book stating what fragments were taken from it. In soaking off leaves of vellum, warm water must on no account be used, as it causes the vellum to shrink up. Indeed, it is better to use cold water for everything ; it necessitates a much greater expenditure of time, but it is very much safer.

If the fragments are not of much importance, they should not be taken from the binding, for the removal, however carefully done, must tend to hurt the book. It will be sufficient to make a note of their existence for reference at any time. When important fragments are extracted, it is best to bind them up separately and place them on the shelves, and not keep them loose in boxes or drawers, or pasted into scrap-books. For many typographical purposes the fragment is as useful as the complete book.

In conclusion, a word may be said on the methods of treating and preserving old bindings. In the first place, a binding should never be touched or repaired unless it is absolutely necessary ; and if it is of any value, it should be kept in a plain case. These cases should always be made so that the side opens, not, as is more usual, open only at the end, for then every time the book is taken out the sides are rubbed. If they are made in the form of a book with overlapping edges, they can be lettered on the back and stand on the shelves with other books.

If it is necessary that the binding should be repaired, nothing should be destroyed. If, for example, a portion of the back has been lost, what remains should be kept, and not an entirely new back put on. In repairing calf bindings, morocco should be used, as near the colour of the original as possible, and the grain should be pressed out. The old end-papers should, of course, be retained, and nothing of any kind destroyed which affords a link in the history of the book. No attempt should be made to ornament the repaired portion so as to resemble the rest of the binding; it serves no useful purpose, and takes away considerably from the good appearance and value of what is left, for a binding which has been 'doctored' must always be looked upon with some mistrust.

An old calf book should never be varnished; it does not really help to preserve it, and it gives it an unsightly appearance, besides tending to fill up the more delicate details in the ornamentation. Some writers recommend that old bindings should be rubbed with vaseline or other similar preparations. Nothing is better than good furniture cream or paste. A few drops should be lightly rubbed on the binding with a piece of flannel; it should be left for a few minutes, until nearly dry, and then rubbed with a soft dry cloth. Not only does this soften the leather and prevent it getting friable, but it puts an excellent surface and polish upon it, quite unlike that produced by varnish. When a binding is in good condition and the surface not rubbed through, it is best to leave it alone; if any dusting or rubbing has to be done, it should be done with a silk handkerchief.

CHAPTER XIII.

THE COLLECTING AND DESCRIBING OF EARLY PRINTED BOOKS.

IT is exactly one hundred years since Panzer, " the one true naturalist among general bibliographers," published the first volume of his *Annales Typographici*, and in this period two distinct methods of bibliography have grown up.

The more popular, generally associated with the name of Dibdin, treats specimens of early printing merely as curiosities, valuable only according to their rarity or intrinsic worth, or for some individual peculiarity found in them.

The other method, of which Panzer was the first practical exponent, was called by Henry Bradshaw the Natural History method. Each press must be looked upon as a *genus*, and each book as a *species*, and the more or less close connection of the different members of the family must be traced by the characters which they present to our observation. Bradshaw's own work is the best example of this method, and a beginner can follow no better model than the papers which he wrote on early printing.

In collecting or studying early printed books, one of the most fatal and common mistakes is the under-

taking of too much. The day is past when one man
will set himself to compile such works as Hain's
Repertorium Bibliographicum, or that very much
greater book, Panzer's *Annales Typographici;* both
wonderful achievements, but unfinished and imperfect.
No one who has not had practical experience can
imagine the amount of information which can be
obtained by taking a small subject and working at it
carefully; or conversely, the amount of careful study
and research that is requisite to work a small subject
properly.

Take as examples Blades' *Life of Caxton* and
Edmond's *Aberdeen Printers*, the two best monographs we possess. They contain a very great deal
of most careful work, and sufficient material to enable
any one who desires to study those particular subjects
to do so thoroughly.

In collecting, in the same way, a beginner who
wishes his collection to be of real value should not
be too catholic in his tastes, but confine his attention
to one subject. A collection of fifty miscellaneous
fifteenth-century books has not, as a rule, more
interest than may be associated with the individual
books. But take a collection of fifty books printed
in one town, or by one printer. Each book is then
a part of a series, and obtains a value on that account
over and above its own individual rarity or interest.

The arrangement and cataloguing of early printed
books is a part of the subject which presents many
difficulties. In many great collections, these books,

for purposes of bibliographical study, are absolutely lost. They are not bought, at any rate not once in twenty cases, for their literary value, but simply and solely as specimens of early printing or curiosities. But, having been bought, they are treated as any other book bought solely for its literary value, and in no other way, *i.e.* they are catalogued under the author or concealed in mazes of cross-reference. If such books are to be bought at all, they should surely be treated in some way which would enable them to fulfil the object for which they were acquired.

In the University Library, Cambridge, the fifteenth-century books are all placed together arranged under countries according to size, with a press-mark indicating the country, the size, and the consecutive number. Thus any new acquisition can be added, and placed at once without disarranging the order on the shelves. Any further subdivision, as, for instance, under towns, is impracticable on the shelves, but must be done on paper.

The catalogue slips can then be arranged under towns and printers, so that any one wishing to study the productions of a particular town or printer can at once obtain all the books of the particular class in the library. If he knows his books by the author's name, they can be found from the general catalogue of the library. In private collections, the number of books is, as a rule, so small that they can be arranged in any order without trouble.

In describing an early printed book, great care

should always be taken not to confuse what is common to all examples of the book with what is specially the peculiarity of an individual copy. The description should always be in two parts, the first general and the second particular. The first part should give the place, the date, the name of the printer, the size, an exact collation ; the second, an account of the binding, a list of the earlier owners, the imperfections, if any, and similar information.

As regards the place, there does not yet seem to be any fixed rule as to the form in which it should be written, whether in Latin or in English. Many of the older bibliographies having been written in Latin, and the colophons of the majority of early books being in the same language, we have grown familiar with the Latin forms of many names. But now that more books are being written in English, it seems more sensible to use the English forms. The pedantic habit of writing the name in the vernacular, as Köln for Cologne, Genève for Geneva, or Kjøbenhavn for Copenhagen, should be avoided ; it simply tends to confuse, and serves no useful purpose. The great aim of a bibliographical description should be to give the fullest information in the most concise and clear form. Since English books are presumably written for English readers, it is best they should be written in English, and the exhibition of superfluous learning in the manner is almost always a sign of a want of necessary learning in the matter.

The date should always be given in Arabic figures ;

and if there is any peculiarity in the form of the date as it occurs in the book, it should be added between brackets. The day of the month, when it is given in the colophon, should always be put down in the description, as it is often of great importance. In countries where the new year began in March we are apt to get confused with the dates, and forget, for example, that the 20th of January 1490 is later than the 20th of December 1490.

The beginning of the year varied in different countries, and often in different towns. The four most usual times for its commencement were : Christmas Day (December 25), the day of the Circumcision (January 1), the day of the Conception (March 25), and the day of the Resurrection (Easter Day). The 25th of March was, on the whole, most common ; but in dating any book exactly, the rule for the particular town where it was printed should be ascertained.

An approximate date should always be supplied to the description of an undated book ; but this date should not be a mere haphazard conjecture, but should be determined by an examination of the characteristics of the book, and comparison with dated books from the same press, so that the date that is ascribed is merely another expression for the characteristics noticed in the book. It is only after careful study that accurate dates can be ascribed to books of a particular press, and monographs on particular printers must be consulted when it is possible.

On the question of sizes there seem to be many opinions. There was originally no doubt on the subject, and there is no reason for any doubt now.

There are two opposing elements at work, size and form. Originally, when all paper was handmade, and did not vary very much in measurement, books were spoken of as folio, quarto, octavo, etc., according to the folding of the sheet; and these terms apply to the folding of the sheet. In the present century, when paper is made by machinery, and made to any size, the folding cannot be taken as a criterion, and the various sizes are determined by measurement, the old terms, applicable only to the size by folding, being retained. What has evidently led to all this confusion is the application of the same terms to two different things.

In describing old books, the old form size should be used, being the only one which does not vary. Under the other notation, a cut-down copy of a book in quarto becomes an octavo, and thus two editions are made out of one.

The size of an old book is very simply recognised by holding up a page to the light. Certain white lines, called wire-marks, will be noticed, occurring, as a rule, about an inch apart, and running at right angles to the fine lines. These wire-lines are perpendicular in a folio, octavo, 32mo, and horizontal in a quarto and 16mo. In a 12mo, as the name implies, the sheet is folded in twelve; and in the earlier part at least of the sixteenth century this was done in such a way that the wire-lines are perpendicular ; the height of the sheet forming two pages, as is the case in an octavo, while the width is divided into six, instead of four as in an octavo. The later habit has been to fold the sheet differently, the height of the sheet forming the width of four pages, and the width of the sheet the height of three pages ; consequently the wire-lines are horizontal. Among early printed books the 12mo is a very uncommon form ; quartos are most numerous, and after them folios.

It should always be remembered that the signature has nothing whatever to do with the size. It is merely a guide to the binder to show him how many leaves go to the quire, and the order in which they come. The binder found it convenient to have his quires of from eight to twelve leaves each, and the quires were thus made up whether the book was folio, quarto, or octavo. Let us assume, for example, that the quires were to consist of eight leaves each, then each quire of the folio book contained four sheets, of the quarto book two sheets, and of the octavo book one sheet. A book on Book Collecting, lately published, gives the following extraordinary remarks on finding the size :—" The leaves must be counted between signature and signature, and then if there are two leaves the book is a folio, if four a 4to, if eight an 8vo, if twelve a 12mo, etc. . . . I should advise the young collector to count the leaves between signature and signature, and to abide by the result, regardless of all the learned arguments of specialists." The absolute folly of these remarks on the sizes of books will be apparent to any one who has seen an old book. The earliest folios printed in Germany and Italy are in quires of ten leaves, *i.e.* there are ten leaves between signature and signature; in the majority of early folios there are eight. Again, there is no folio book in existence among early books (excepting the block-books, which are in a class apart) with only two leaves to the signature.

Wynkyn de Worde made up many of his quartos in quires of eight and four leaves alternately; most early 16mos were made up in quires of eight leaves, and had therefore two signatures to each complete sheet. In the same way many 24mos were made up in quires of twelve leaves. All these books would be wrongly described by counting the leaves between the signatures; in fact, that method comes right by accident only in the case of some octavos and a few 12mos and 16mos.[1]

The collation of a book is the enumeration of the number of leaves according to the way in which they are arranged in quires, and this collation should be given whether the quires are signed or not. If there are signatures, there can be no difficulty in counting the number of leaves which go to each quire; but when there are no signatures, as is the case with most

---

[1] On the subject of the sizes of old books, the reader would do well to consult the *Athenæum*, 1888, vol. ii. pp. 600, 636, 673, 706, and 744, where some instructive and amusing letters will be found. A further series of letters relating generally to the same subject appeared in the same paper in the early part of 1889.

books before 1475, the collation is a more difficult matter. The first thing to be looked at, if the book has no MS. signatures, is the sewing, which shows us the centre of the quire,[1] and we can then count from sewing to sewing. This gives us only the halves of two quires ; we must then have recourse to the water-marks. In a folio, if one leaf has a watermark, the corresponding leaf which forms the other half of the sheet has none. Again, in a quarto, corresponding leaves have either no watermark, or each half a one. Judging from the sewing and the watermarks, there is rarely any difficulty in making out the collation, the first and last quires being the most difficult to deter-mine with accuracy ; the others present no difficulty. It is thus always best to settle the arrangement of the interior quires first, and work from them to the outer ones, which are more likely to be mutilated.

This method of collation by the watermarks is very often useful for detecting made up copies. For instance, in the copy of the thirty-six line Bible in the British Museum, the first and last leaf of the first quire have each a watermark, showing absolutely that one of the two leaves (in this case the first) has been inserted from another copy.

In many old books which have been rebound, the

---

[1] It was the custom of many binders in the earlier part of the present century, when they had to rebind an old book, to separate all the leaves and then fix them together in convenient sections, entirely ignoring the original "make up." A very large number of books in the British Museum were thus misbound, and even the celebrated Codex Alex-andrinus was treated in this way.

outside pages of the quire are very much smoother
and more polished than the rest, and may thus be
distinguished by touch.   This, though a pretty certain
test, may mislead, if the book has been misbound,
and should only be used in conjunction with the other
methods.   A little practical work will soon enable the
beginner to find for himself various small points, all
of which, though hardly worthy of a lengthy description, are useful in giving information, but are only
useful when they have been acquired by experience.

In giving an account of a fifteenth century book,
a reference should always be made to Hain's *Repertorium Bibliographicum.*   If Hain gives a full
description, and such description is correct, it will be
sufficient for all purposes to quote the number in
Hain.   Almost all the books fully described in that
work have an asterisk prefixed to their number, that
being the sign that Hain had himself collated the
book ; and in quoting from him the asterisk should
never be omitted.

The title and colophon should always be given in
extenso, the end of each line in the original being
marked by an upright stroke (|).   The abbrevia-
tions should be exactly copied.   Notice must always
be taken of blank leaves which are part of the book.
The number of lines to the page, the presence or
absence of signatures, all such technical minutiæ
must be noted down.

In fact, the object of a good bibliographical description is to give as clearly and concisely as possible

all the information which can be derived from an examination of the book itself.

The individual history of a book is of the utmost importance, and should never be ignored. On this subject I cannot do better than quote some words of Henry Bradshaw, applicable more to manuscripts than to printed books, but which explain the writer's careful method, and practically exhaust all that has to be said on the subject.

" These notes, moreover, illustrate the method on which I have worked for many years, the method which alone brings me satisfaction, whether dealing with printed books or manuscripts. It is briefly this : to work out the history of the volume from the present to the past ; to peel off, as it were, every accretion, piece by piece, entry by entry, making each contribute its share of evidence of the book's history backwards from generation to generation ; to take note of every entry which shows either use, or ownership, or even the various changes of library arrangement, until we get back to the book itself as it left the original scriptorium or the hands of the scribe ; noting how the book is made up, whether in 4-sheet, 5-sheet, or 6-sheet quires, or otherwise ; how the quires are numbered and marked for the binder ; how the corrector has done his work, leaving his certificate on the quire, leaf or page, or not, as the case may be ; how the rubricator has performed his part ; what kind of handwriting the scribe uses ; and, finally, to what country or district all these pieces of evidence point.

. . . The quiet building up of facts, the habit of patiently watching a book, and listening while it tells you its own story, must tend to produce a solid groundwork of knowledge, which alone leads to that sober confidence before which both negative assumption and ungrounded speculation, however brilliant, must ultimately fall."

INDEX OF PRINTERS AND PLACES.

ABBEVILLE, 90, 91.
Abingdon, 182, 183.
Alban's, St., 140.
Albi, 71, 90.
Aldus, 69, 70.
Alopa, F. de, 75.
Alost, 97, 101, 102, 103, 104.
Alyat, A., 189.
Amorbach, J., 58, 189.
Andreæ, J., 112.
Andrieu, M., 93.
Angers, 88, 89.
Angoulême, 93.
Antwerp, 103, 108, 111, 112, 134, 171, 172, 181, 190.
Appentegger, L., 114.
Arndes, S., 122.
Ascensius, J. B., *see* Badius.
Audenarde, 110, 111.
Augsburg, 51, 52, 56, 61, 148.
Avignon, 19, 78, 80, 94.
Azzoguidi, B., 72.

BADIUS, J., 86, 174, 177.
Bamberg, 24, 39, 43, 45, 47.
Bamler, 41, 51.
Barbier, J., 143, 144.
Barcelona, 114, 115, 117, 121, 148.
Barmentlo, P., 110.
Barnes, J., 156.
Basle, 23, 57, 58, 111, 172.
Bechtermuntze, H., 34, 35, 36, 37.

Bechtermuntze, N., 36, 37, 54, 55.
Bedill, J., 143.
Belfortis, A., 65, 72.
Bellaert, 112.
Bellescullée, P., 89.
Benedictis, de, 72.
Bergman de Olpe, P., 51.
Beromunster, 58.
Bertolf von Hanau, *see* B. Ruppel.
Berton, J., 94.
Besançon, 92.
Beverley, 178.
Bois-le-duc, 112.
Bollcaert, J., 190.
Bologna, 72.
—— S. de, 119.
Bonhomme, P., 83.
Botel, H., 115.
Bourgeois, J. le, 92.
Bouyer, J., 89.
Braem, C., 104.
Braga, 121.
Brandis, L., 57.
Brasichella, G. de, 70.
Breda, J. de, 110.
Bréhant-Loudéac, 90, 91.
Breslau, 57.
Brito, J., 106, 107.
Bruges, 105, 106, 111, 126, 136.
Brun, P., 115.
Brunswick, 157.
Brussels, 107, 108.
Bruxella, A. de, 76.

Buckinck, A., 63, 64.
Burgos, 117.
Butz, L., 114.
Buyer, B., 87.

CADAROSSIA, D. de, 79.
Caen, 89, 90.
Cagliari, 119.
Calafati, N., 117.
Caliergi, Z., 70, 76.
Cambridge, 180, 194, 197.
Carner, A., 72.
Castaldi, P., 59.
Caxton, W., 48, 49, 84, 105, 125,
  126, 127, 128, 129, 130, 131,
  132, 133, 134, 135, 136, 137,
  138, 139, 141, 142, 148, 157,
  159, 160, 165, 166, 167, 171,
  172, 191, 192, 196.
Cayllaut, A., 84.
Cennini, B., 74.
Chablis, 88, 89, 91.
Chalcondylas, D., 75.
Châlons, 93.
Chambéry, 90.
Chardella, S. N., 66.
Chartres, 90.
Chepman, W., 174.
Cividad di Friuli, 77.
Clemens Sacerdos, 68.
Cluni, 93.
Cock, G., 114.
Coeffin, M., 184.
Colini, J., 91.
Cologne, 42, 47, 48, 49, 50, 51,
  91, 96, 108, 126, 127, 149, 154,
  155, 169, 171, 172.
Copenhagen, 109, 122.
Copland, R., 129, 142.
Coria, 118.
Cosselhac, A. de, 79.
Coster, L. J., 95, 98.
Crantz, M., 81, 83,

Cremona, 77.
Crès, J., 91, 92.
Creusner, F., 53.

DACHAVER, 88.
Dale, H. van den, 111.
Davidson, T., 176.
Daygne, C., 175.
Delft, 109.
De Marnef, 175.
Deventer, 109, 110, 172.
Dijon, 93.
Dinckmut, C., 16, 57.
Dôle, 92, 93.
Dorne, J., 157.
Dortas, A., 120.
Drach, P., 37, 54, 55.
Durandas, J., 90.
Durham, 188.

EDINBURGH, 174, 175, 176.
Eggestein, H., 39, 41, 42, 56,
  188.
Egmondt, F., 171.
Eichstadt, 55.
Eliezer, 120.
Eltvil, 34, 36, 37, 54.
Elyas, C., 57.
Embrun, 93.
Erfurth, 21.
Esslingen, 55, 73.
Eustace, G., 85.
Exeter, 184.
Eysenhut, J., 11.

FABRI, J., 122, 123.
Faques, G., 7, 197.
—— R., 197.
Faro, 121.
Fernandez, A., 113, 114.
Ferrara, 65, 72, 73.
Ferrose, G., 79.
Fèvre, G. le, 84.

Flandrus, M., 114.
Florence, 72, 74, 75, 76.
Fogel, J., 188.
Foligno, 71.
Forestier, J. le, 92.
Foucquet, R., 91.
Francour, J. de, 119.
Frankfort, 20, 32.
Frederick of Basle, 117.
Frees, F., 177, 178.
—— G., 177.
Friburger, M., 81, 83.
Friedberg, P. de, 33.
Froben, J., 58.
Fust, John, 23, 24, 25, 26, 46, 47, 80.
Fyner, C., 55, 56.

GACHET, J., 180.
Gallus, U., *see* Hahn, U.
Gaver, J., 143.
Geneva, 58.
Gérard, P., 91.
Gerardus de Lisa, 76.
Gering, U., 81, 83.
Gerona, 114, 116, 117.
Ghemen, G. van, 109, 122, 179.
Ghent, 111, 112.
Gherlinc, J., 121.
Ghotan, B., 123.
Giunta, 70.
Godard, G., 85.
Goes, H., 177, 178, 179.
—— M. van der, 111, 134.
Gops, G., 50, 51.
Gossin, J., 106.
Gotz, N., 50, 91, 127, 198.
Gouda, 108, 109, 179.
Goupil, R., 184.
Goupillières, 93.
Gourmont, G., 86.
Gradibus, J. and S., 89.
Granada, 119.

Grenoble, 93.
Gruninger, J., 43.
Guldenschaff, J., 51, 149.
Gurniel, J. de, 115.
Gutenberg, John, 22, 23, 24, 25, 31, 34, 35, 36, 40, 46, 47, 52, 53, 57, 71, 82, 96.

H., I., 143, 144.
Haarlem, 97, 98, 99, 112.
Hagembach, P., 114.
Haghe, I., 183.
Hahn, U., 64, 65, 66.
Hardouyn, G., 85.
Harsy, N. de, 92.
Hasselt, 110.
Heerstraten, E. van der, 104, 172.
Hees, W., 102.
Helyas de Louffen, 58.
Hereford, 180, 183.
Hermann de Stalhoen, 32.
Hermonymus, G., 20.
Hertzog, J., 171, 172.
Higman, J., 84, 139.
Hijst, J. and C., 55.
Hochfeder, C., 91.
Hohenwang, L., 56.
Homery, C., 35, 36.
Hopyl, W., 174.
Hostingue, L., 175, 184.
Hug de Goppingen, J., 56.
Hunt, T., 151, 155.
Hurus, P., 114.
Husner, G., 43.

JACOBI, H., 156, 193.
Jaen, 119.
Janszoon, L., *see* Coster, L. J.
Jardina, G. de la, 79.
Jenson, N., 48, 66, 67, 68, 80, 96.
John de Colonia, 50, 69.
John of Speyer, 66.

KACHELOFFEN, C., 16.
Kaetz, P., 181.
Kaiser, P., 82, 83, 89.
Keffer, H., 23, 35, 52.
Keller, A., 189.
—— J., 148.
Kerver, T., 85.
Kesler, N., 111.
Ketelaer, N., 102.
Keysere, A. de, 110.
Knoblochzer, J., 43.
Koburger, A., 53, 189.
Koelhoff, J., 50.
Kuilenburg, 15, 16, 104, 112.
Kyrfoth, C., 156.

LANDEN, J., 155.
Lantenac, 93.
Lausanne, 58.
Lauxius, D., 174.
Lavagna, P. de, 73.
Laver, G., 63.
Lavingen, 56.
Lecompte, N., 171.
Leempt, G. de, 102, 110, 112.
Leeu, G., 108, 109, 111, 112, 171, 172.
Leipzig, 16, 20.
Leiria, 120, 121.
Lerida, 115.
Lettou, J., 129, 160, 161, 197, 198.
Levet, P., 84, 139.
Leyden, 109, 112.
Lila, B. de, 118.
Limoges, 94.
Lisbon, 120.
Loeffs, R., 104.
Loeslein, P., 69.
London, 6, 107, 141, 143, 145, 156, 160, 161, 178, 181, 188, 197, 198.
Louvain, 15, 103, 104, 172, 190.

Loys, J., 184.
Lubeck, 57, 122, 123.
Ludwig zu Ulm, 10, 56.
Lyons, 72, 86, 87, 94, 175.

MACHLINIA, W. de, 107, 161, 162, 163, 164, 165, 166.
Maçon, 93.
Madrid, 119.
Mainz, 21, 23, 25, 31, 32, 33, 34, 35, 36, 37, 38, 39, 44, 46, 47, 52, 58, 60, 67, 71, 82, 95, 96, 100, 101.
Mansion, C., 105, 106, 127.
Manthen, J., 69.
Mantua, 77.
Marchant, G., 84.
Marienthal, 37, 38, 108.
Martens, Th., 103, 104, 112.
Marti, B., 117.
Martinez, A., 114.
Mayer, H., 88, 118, 119.
Maynyal, G., 133, 171.
Melchior de Stanheim, 52.
Mentelin, J., 39, 40, 41, 42, 43.
Merseburg, 57.
Metlinger, P., 92.
Metz, 90, 91.
Milan, 68, 72, 73, 74.
Milner, U., 178, 179, 180.
Monreale, 77.
Monserrat, 119.
Monterey, 119.
Moravia, V. de, 120.
Moravus, M., 161.
Morelli, 89.
Morin, M., 92.
Murcia, 118.
Myllar, A., 174, 175.

NANTES, 93.
Naples, 72, 76, 161.

Narbonne, 93.
Nassou, H. de, 104.
Nijmegen, 110, 112.
Norins, J., 189.
Notary, J., 141, 143, 144, 145, 146, 193.
Novacivitate, G. de, 91.
Numeister, J., 71, 90.
Nuremberg, 10, 11, 23, 43, 52, 53, 91, 108.

ODENSEE, 121, 122.
Orleans, 93.
Orrier, B. van, 111.
Os, G. de, 109, 137, 139, 140.
—— P. van, 110.
Oxford, 125, 134, 147, 148, 149, 150, 151, 152, 153, 154, 155, 156, 182, 187, 192.

P., I., 190.
Padua, 77.
Paffroed, R., 110.
Palma, 117.
Palmart, L., 113, 114.
Pannartz, A., 59, 60, 61, 62, 63, 64, 65.
Paris, 18, 20, 32, 80, 86, 89, 90, 91, 92, 133, 139, 171, 172, 174, 175, 177, 189.
Parix, J., 88.
Parma, 72, 77.
Passera, G. R. de la, 119.
Pavia, 72, 76.
Périgueux, 94.
Perpignan, 94, 115.
Perusia, 122.
Pfister, A., 24, 25, 43, 44, 45, 46, 47.
Philippus Petri, 68.
Picheng, 2.
Pictor, B., 69.
Pigouchet, P., 85.

Pistoia, D. de, 74.
Poitiers, 89.
Porres, J. de, 119.
Portilia, A., 72.
Pré, J. du, 84, 90, 91, 92, 94.
Printer of Augustinus de Fide, 50, 127.
—— Dictys, 50.
—— Historia S. Albani, 50.
Promentour, 58.
Provins, 94.
Puerto, A. del, 114.
Pynson, R., 92, 145, 156, 163, 165, 166, 167, 168, 169, 170, 176, 193.

QUENTELL, H., 51, 169.
Quijoue, E., 90.

R PRINTER, 42, 43.
Raem de Berka, G. ten, 149.
Ratdolt, E., 29, 69, 148.
Ravescot, L. de, 104.
Redman, R., 170.
Regnault, F., 85, 92.
Rennes, 90.
Reuchlin, 20.
Reutlingen, 56.
Reüwick, E., 33.
Reynes, J., 193.
Reyser, M., 55.
Richard, J., 92.
Richel, B., 58.
Richenbach, J., 188.
Riessinger, S., 76.
Roca, L. de, 118.
Rodt, B., *see* Ruppel.
Rome, 61, 64, 65.
Rood, T., 149, 151, 154, 155.
Rosembach, 115.
Rostock, 108.
Rouen, 90, 91, 92, 166, 167, 168, 172, 175, 176, 177, 184.

Rouge, G. le, 89, 91.
—— P. le, 84, 89, 91.
Roy, G. le, 87.
—— J. le, 93.
Ruppel, B., 23, 57, 58.
Rusch d'Ingwiller, A., 40, 42.
Rychard, T., 182.

St. Alban's, 140, 157, 158, 159.
St. Maartensdyk, 110.
Salamanca, 116.
Salins, 90.
San Cucufat, 118.
Saragossa, 114.
Saxonia, N. de, 120.
Schenck, P., 89.
Schiedam, 112.
Schleswig, 122.
Schœffer, Peter, 22, 23, 24, 25,
    27, 29, 30, 31, 32, 33, 34, 35,
    47, 48, 58, 80.
Schoensperger, J., 52.
Schott, M., 40.
Schussler, J., 52, 61.
Scolar, J., 156, 182.
Scot, J., 143.
Scotus, O., 69.
Segorbe, 116.
Segura, B., 114.
Sensenschmidt, J., 47, 52.
Seville, 88, 114, 115.
Shoenhoven, 112.
Siberch, J. L. de, 180, 181.
Snell, J., 121, 122.
Solidi, J., 89.
Sorg, A., 52.
Spindeler, N., 115.
Spire, 37, 53, 54, 55.
Sporer, Hans, 10, 11.
Spyess, W., 36, 37.
Stockholm, 122, 123, 124.
Stoll, J., 82, 83, 89.
Story, J., 176.

Strasburg, 22, 23, 39, 40, 41, 43,
    55, 76, 96.
Subiaco, 31, 52, 59, 60, 61, 62.
Sursee, 58.
Sweynheym, C., 59, 60, 61, 62,
    63, 64, 65.

Talleur, G. le, 92, 166, 168,
    175.
Taro, 121.
Tarragona, 115, 119.
Tavistock, 182.
Theodoricus, 154, 155.
Ther Hoernen, A., 50, 108, 149,
    155.
Thorne, J., 157.
Toledo, 114, 116.
Tolosa, 88, 118, 119.
Toro, 121.
Torresani, A. de, 70.
Toulouse, 87, 118, 119.
Tours, 93.
Trechsel, J., 86.
Tréguier, 90.
Treveris, P., 157.
Treves, 91.
Treviso, 72, 76.
Trogen, 58.
Troyes, 89, 90, 91.
Turre, J. de, 89.

Udina, 77.
Ulm, 16, 56, 57, 61.
Ulric and Afra, Monastery of, 52.
Urach, 56.
Utrecht, 15, 16, 97, 99, 101, 102,
    103, 104, 107.

Valdarfer, C., 68, 73.
Valence, 94.
Valenciennes, 94.
Valentia, 113, 114, 118.
Valladolid, 115, 119.